1 MONTH OF
FREE
READING

at

www.ForgottenBooks.com

By purchasing this book you are eligible for one month membership to ForgottenBooks.com, giving you unlimited access to our entire collection of over 1,000,000 titles via our web site and mobile apps.

To claim your free month visit:

www.forgottenbooks.com/free532985

ISBN 978-0-331-96121-8
PIBN 10532985

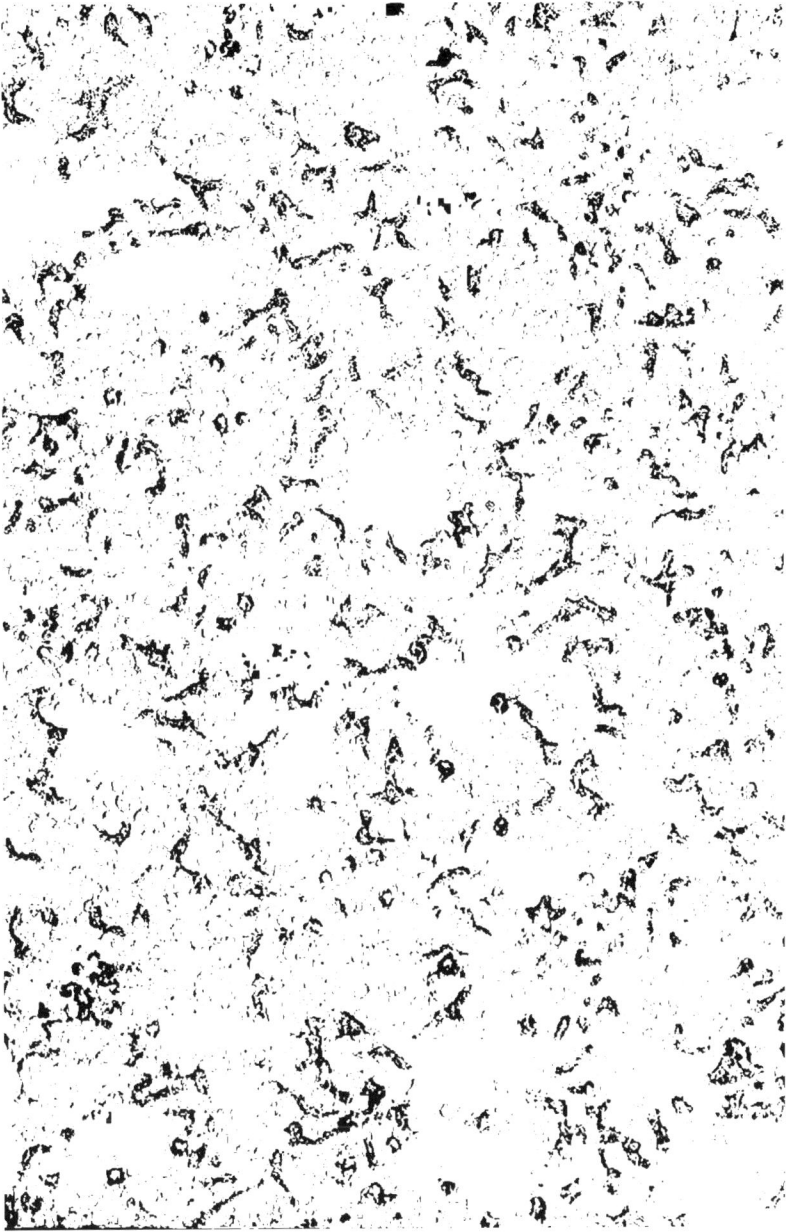

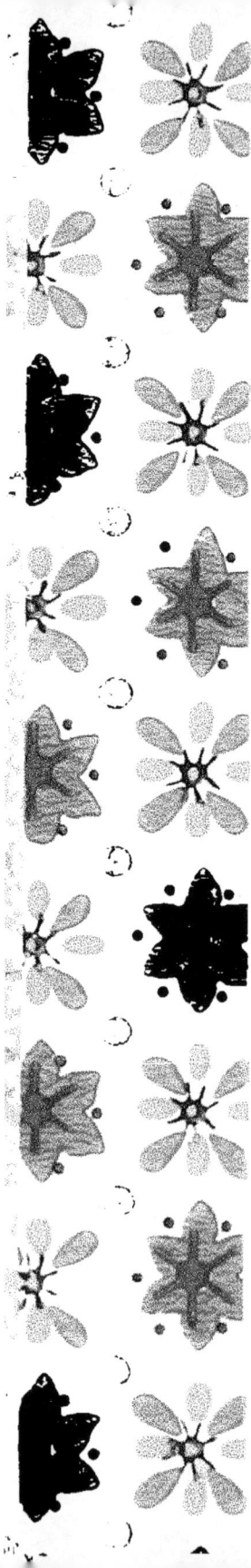

Jeremias van Rensselaer

AMERICAN HISTORICAL MAGAZINE

VOL. 2   JANUARY, 1907.   NO. I

THE VAN RENSSELAER FAMILY.

BY W. W. SPOONER.

OF the early Dutch colonial families the Van Rensselaers were the first to acquire a great landed estate in America under the "patroon" system; they were among the first, after the English conquest of New Netherland, to have their possessions erected into a "manor," antedating the Livingstons and Van Cortlandts in this particular; and they were the last to relinquish their ancient prescriptive rights and to part with their hereditary demesnes under the altered social and political conditions of modern times. So far as an aristocracy, in the strict understanding of the term, may be said to have existed under American institutions—and it is an undoubted historical fact that a quite formal aristocratic society obtained throughout the colonial period and for some time subsequently, especially in New York,—the Van Rensselaers represented alike its highest attained privileges, its most elevated organization, and its most dignified expression. They were, in the first place, nobles in the old country, which cannot be said of any of the other manorial families of New York, although several of these claimed gentle descent. Thus in becoming patroons and later manorial lords in America, the Van Rensselaers but enjoyed an extension in kind (though scarcely in degree) of aristocratic dignities which had already been theirs for generations. Measured by the standard of American antiquity, they take precedence of every other New York family of present consequence, their patroonship having been created in 1631, only eight years after the first permanent settlement of the Dutch on Manhattan Island. Their territorial possessions were from the first of grand dimensions—some twenty-four by forty-eight miles,—surpassing many a European principality. And finally their special privileges—by which we identify and recognize a regularly established, as distinguished from a socially improvised, aristocracy—were the highest accorded to any family in America, either under the Dutch regime or the English. The Van Rensselaer domains (or, more correctly, dominions), as originally acquired by the founder óf the house with the sanction of the government of Holland, constituted a distinct colony, not subject in any manner to the political control or jurisdiction of the general administration of New Netherland; and indeed their independence was so sharply defined that Governor Stuyvesant, in a dispute with the Van Rensselaer director regarding territorial rights, could find no other recourse than an act of war. When the Dutch patroonship was converted into an English manor, the peculiar privileges of the Van Rensselaers suffered no material abridgment, but in certain respects were given a more pronounced character. The manor, or "lordship," was formally set aside, by the terms of the English grant, as a separate political entity; and while the powers of its proprietors underwent some modifications, as was inevitable with the change from Dutch to British laws, they were conceded all the very considerable privileges and functions belonging to manor lords in England, such as exclusive police power within their territories, appointment and control of the necessary officials, administration of justice in ordinary causes, and the right of advowson. As a further enlargement of the dignity of the manor, its inhabitants were given the right to elect and send a special deputy to the general assembly of the province; and, as a matter of course, the deputy chosen was invariably either the head of the family or his immediate personal representative. Again, the position of the Van Rensselaer Family as one of the foremost in the aristocratic order in America was secured so long as that order should endure by the application of the law of primogeniture, requiring the perpetual transmission of the entire landed estate in the eldest male line; a law which prevented the dispersal of the property among the younger branches, and imposed upon the direct succeeding line an obligation to maintain the family pretensions upon a plane and in a manner befitting the undivided inheritance.

The exceptional position conferred upon the Van Rensselaer Family, and for generations sustained, by virtue of its great proprietary estate, is naturally the most conspicuous fact in its history. The patroonship or manor of Rensselaerswyck, as originally erected, was diminished at various times in the seventeenth and eighteenth centuries by alienations; including a considerable tract ceded to the city of Albany, two other large cessions (the "Coeyman's Tract" and an extensive strip transferred to the state of Massachusetts), and a territory of some sixty thousand acres, constituting the "Lower" or "Claverack" Manor, with other lands vested in the younger branch of the family, as its share, at the time of the settlement of the primogenitureship, in the reign of Queen Anne. Notwithstanding these alienations, the manor was still the greatest hereditary property in the state of New York, and as adjusted on its final territorial basis it continued, without further reduction, until toward the middle of the nineteenth century. Throughout this period of two centuries its character as a strictly private estate remained unchanged; and although the formal privileges of civil authority which belonged to its early proprietors, as well as the principle of primogeniture, were abolished in the Revolution, the ancient features of a single headship and exclusive ownership of the soil on the one hand, and a semi-feudal tenantship on the other, were preserved to the last.

From association with public events of great importance

and dramatic interest between the years 1839 and 1846, the Van Rensselaer name became identified, even more promiuently than before, with the history of the state of New York. This is not the place for any examination of the merits of the so-called "Anti-Rent" controversy, nor is any special presentation of the Van Rensselaer side of the dispute required, even in a quite formal and sympathetic sketch of the family. It may be remarked that all the writers on that exciting and notable political episode who rank as authorities have given tolerably proportionate attention to the considerations in favor of the Van Rensselaers, and, on the whole, have dealt with the subject dispassionately.

The Van Rensselaers in Holland

The antiquity of the Van Rensselaer Family in Holland is established by many indutiable evidences. The late Eugene Schuyler, a historical writer of high reputation, during a visit to Holland (1879) made researches concerning the origin of the Van Rensselaers, visiting the principal localities connected with their name. They are traceable, he says, to a manor still called Rensselaer, which is situated about three miles southeast of the village of Nykerk in Guelderland (Holland). "It was originally a *Reddergoed*, the possession of which conferred nobility. The estate is now only a farm, all the old buildings having lately been taken down. They were covered with gables and weathercocks of the arms and crest of the family. There is scarcely a church in Guelderland that did not have somewhere the Van Rensselear arms on the tombstones, either alone or quartered with others."

In the Orphan Asylum at Nykerk, established in 1638, there is still preserved a large picture, representing the founders and regents of that institution; among whom was the Jonkheer Jan Van Rensselaer. He is attired in the dress of the Dutch nobility of that day, and above his head are shown the familiar arms of his family.[1]

The branch of the Hollandish family from which the progenitor of the American Van Rensselaers sprang has been traced back for four antecedent generations, as follows:

I. *Hendrick Woters Van Rensselaer,* married Swene Van Indyck of Hemegseet. Issue: i. *Johannes Hendrick Van Rensselaer,* married Derykebia Van Luxoel. ii. Giertruy Van Rensselaer, married Advocate Swaaskens. iii. Walter Hendrick Van Rensselaer. iv. Anna Van Rensselaer, married Mr. Bygimp. v. Betye Van Rensselaer, married Mr. Noggen.

II. *Johannes Hendrick Van Rensselaer,* married Derykebia Van Luxoel. Issue: i. *Kiliaen Van Rensselaer,* married Nelle Van Vrenoken. ii. Walter Jans Van Rensselaer.

III. *Kiliaen Van Rensselaer,* married Nelle Van Vrenoken. Issue: i. *Hendrick Van Rensselaer,* married Maria Pasraat. ii. Engeltie Van Rensselaer, married Gerrit William Van Patten. iii. Claas Van Rensselaer, married Jacobina Van Schrassens. iv. Johannes Van Rensselaer, married Sandrina Van Erp, styled Waredenburgh.

IV. *Hendrick Van Rensselaer,* married Maria Pasraat.

---

1. Armorial bearings of the Van Rensselaers: Gules, a cross moline argent. *Crest*—An iron basket (or cresset); out of which issue flames or, above a closed knight's helmet. *Mottoes—Niemand zonder* (No one without it [the cross]), and *Omnibus effulgeo* (I outshine all). De Vermont, in "America Heraldica" (p. 15), gives the crest as "A high basket, from which issue flames; all proper"; but we prefer Mr. Schuyler's description, as he made original investigations in Holland. The Van Rensselaer arms, quartered with the arms of three other families, were emblazoned on one of the stained-glass windows of the old Dutch Church at Albany; underneath them being the following words:

Ian Baptist Van Rensselaer
Directeur Der Colony Rensselaer
Wijck 1656

In early times large iron baskets were placed on castles and at other high points, and fires were kindled in them for purposes of illumination—sometimes in celebration of great events. Hence the Van Rensselaer crest. There is a family tradition that on one of these occasions of extraordinary illumination the Van Rensselaer fires so far outshone all others that the Prince of Orange, in recognition of that circumstance, which corresponded to his estimate of the man, requested the head of the house to substitute for his ancient motto that of *Omnibus effulgeo*—I outshine all.

Issue: i. *Kiliaen Van Rensselaer*, the American patroon, married, 1st, Hillegonda Van Bylaer; 2d, Anna Van Wely, daughter of Johannes and Eleanor (Haeckens) Van Wely. ii. Maria Van Rensselaer, married Rykert Van Twiller.

Hendrick Van Rensselaer, preceding, was a captain in the Dutch army, and was killed at the siege of Ostend, June 9, 1602. His brother Johannes held the same rank and met the same fate (February 7, 1601). There is a monument to their memory in the Protestant Church of Nykerk. It may be added that the Van Rensselaers were long prominent in civil affairs in Holland, members of the family serving as burgomasters, councillors, treasurers, etc., in many towns.

Although, as will be seen below, the family in Holland has long been extinct in the male line, it is still conspicuously represented there in the female descent.

I

KILIAEN VAN RENSSELAER, only son of Captain Hendrick and Maria (Pasraat) Van Rensselaer, was born in Holland about 1595. He received a careful education, and, succeeding to the headship of the family, took a position of great prominence and influence. He was engaged in the pearl and diamond trade in Amsterdam, and was one of the wealthiest citizens ''at a time when the merchants of Holland, like those of Italy, had become the princes of the land.''

Arriving at manhood's estate at probably the most important and critical period of the history of the United Provinces, when the truce with Spain was drawing to its close and when it was soon to be determined whether the war for independence should be resumed, Van Rensselaer was one of the organizers and original directors of the Dutch West India Company, that famous and powerful auxiliary of the government of the Netherlands in the gigantic contest which shortly ensued. The Dutch West

India Company was chartered in July, 1621, with a capital of seven million florins, being granted exclusive authority and trade privileges in the Dutch possessions of the two Americas, as also of the coast of Africa from the Tropic of Cancer to the Cape of Good Hope. The objects of its creation were, first, to "establish an efficient and aggressive Atlantic maritime power in the struggle with Spain," and second, to colonize, develop, and rule the Dutch American dependencies, of which the splendid country discovered by Henry Hudson in 1609, known as New Netherland and comprehending the present states of New York and New Jersey, was among the most important. Great expectations of commercial and financial advantage being based upon the extensive privileges and imperial powers conceded in the charter, the wealthy merchants of Holland subscribed for the stock with alacrity. The affairs of the company were administered by a directorate known as the "Assembly of the XIX.," from whose members an executive board or college of nine were selected to manage the concerns of New Netherland; and of both these controlling bodies Kiliaen Van Rensselaer was a member.

In the early career of the company he was one of its mainstays, placing several of his vessels at its disposal and twice advancing money to save its credit. His name is conspicuously identified with all its measures of policy, including the original settlement of Manhattan Island, now New York City, in 1623.

As is well known by all students of history, the infant colony of New Netherland languished, the cautious Dutch people having very little inclination to emigrate to wild and uncultivated lands in which no substantial inducements were presented. Within a few years, therefore, it became realized by the company that special measures which would afford a stimulus to colonization were indispensable, and the celebrated plan of "Freedoms and Exemptions" was accordingly devised. Under this plan it was provided that

any member of the company desiring to do so could select
lands in the province of New Netherland, and erect them
into a patroonship under his exclusive personal proprietorship and governmental authority; the sole conditions being
the necessary satisfaction of the natives and the transportation thither, as bona fide settlers, of "fifty souls, upwards of
fifteen years old, one-fourth to be sent during the first
year and the remainder before the expiration of the fourth
year." Upon each patroon was conferred the right "to for-
ever possess and enjoy all the lands lying within the afore-
said limits, together with the fruits, rights, minerals, rivers,
and fountains thereof; as also the chief command and lower
jurisdiction, fishing, fowling, and grinding, to the exclusion
of all others, to be holden from the company as a perpetual
inheritance."

The act of Freedoms and Exemptions was ratified by the
states-general of Holland in June, 1629. Van Rensselaer,
who had borne a principal part in procuring its adoption,
took prompt and energetic steps toward availing himself of
its privileges. He employed as his agent Sebastiaen Jansen
Crol, an officer of the company in command at Fort Orange
(now Albany), who in a series of purchases from the Indians, beginning in 1630 and continuing until 1637, acquired
for him all the land on the west side of the Hudson River
from twelve miles south of Albany to Smack's Island, "at
the mouth of the Mohawk River, stretching two days' jour-
ney into the interior," and also a tract of about the same
dimensions on the east side both north and south of Fort
Orange, and "far into the wilderness." These purchases
comprehended practically the whole of the present counties
of Albany and Rensselaer, the eastern limits extending for
some distance into the state of Massachusetts; and with
subsequent acquisitions Schenectady County, nearly all of
Columbia County, and a part of Greene County were included, the aggregate area of the Van Rensselaer possessions considerably exceeding seven hundred thousand acres.

Besides the Van Rensselaer domain, known as Rens-selaerswyck, two other extensive patroonships, Pavonia and Swaanendael, were organized under the system of Freedoms and Exemptions; but both of these eventually reverted to the ownership of the company, disappearing as private properties.

Rensselaerswyck, on the other hand, was at once placed by its proprietor upon the basis of a fully acquired estate by fulfillment of the condition of settlement. It was duly confirmed to him on the 8th of January, 1631, at a session of the Assembly of the XIX. "holden in Zealand." That he was controlled by perfect good faith, having in view the colonization of his lands and their development for the benefit of his descendants, there is not the slightest doubt. His expenditures in this connection were very heavy, with no possibility of adequate return during his lifetime. Among the items of his disbursements which have been preserved, is one of a cargo of merchandise valued at 12,870 guilders, which he sent to his colonists in 1643 on his own ship, "The Arms of Rensselaerswyck." On the other hand, no present revenue from the lands could be expected, except the insignificant returns from sales of agricultural produce and timber; the patroons being discouraged from engaging in the fur trade (then the chief source of wealth in New Netherland) by restrictions designed to preserve the company's monopoly.

It was Van Rensselaer's wise and far-seeing policy to settle his colonists in close proximity to one another, instead of distributing them widely. By this plan of concentration of settlement he secured for them the advantages of intercourse, of union for defensive purposes, and of progress to the dignity of a community within a reasonable time. The point chosen was the vicinage of Fort Orange, now Albany. The fort was the first trading-post erected by the Dutch on the Hudson after the discovery, and up to Van Rensselaer's time had existed merely as a station incidental to the fur trade, no attempt whatever being made to colonize the country. Here he ''built comfortable houses and ample barns for his tenants; provided them with agricultural implements and livestock; erected saw and grist-mills at convenient places on the larger water-courses, and supplied his store with suitable goods to meet the wants of the colonists.'' ''He maintained a high military and judicial authority, had his own fortresses, planted with his own cannon, manned with his own soldiers, with his own flag waving over them. The courts of his colony were his own courts, where the gravest questions and the highest crimes were cognizable, but with appeals in the more important cases. Justice was administered in his own name. The colonists were his immediate subjects, and took the oath of fealty and allegiance to him.''

Kiliaen Van Rensselaer, in the organization and administration of his colony, as in its purchase, was represented by trusted agents; and there is no record of his having ever visited it, although there is a tradition that he came over for a brief time in 1637. His representatives were men of ability and reputation, whose names are celebrated in the early history of New Netherland. The first vice-director of Rensselaerswyck (who bore the official title of commissary-general and colonial secretary) was Arendt Van Corlaer (or Curler). The equally distinguished Dr. Adriaen Van der Donck, who was the first lawyer in New Netherland, and who subsequently became patroon of Colen Donck (a territory transformed after his time into Philipse Manor, upon which the city of Yonkers now stands), was sent over in 1641 as sheriff and schout-fiscal of Rensselaerswyck, continuing in that capacity until 1646. Another eminent character dispatched to America by Van Rensselaer was Domine Megapolensis, who took charge of the spiritual welfare of the people of Rensselaerswyck, and was the most learned and accomplished of the early Dutch divines in this country.

The death of Kiliaen Van Rensselaer occurred in Holland in 1646.

Married, 1st, Hillegonda Van Bylaer; 2d, Anna Van Wely, daughter of Johannes Van Wely and Eleanor Haeckens. All the sons of Kiliaen Van Rensselaer, except the eldest, were by his second marriage.

Issue:

    1. Johannes Van Rensselaer, second patroon; of whom below

    2. Maria Van Rensselaer, d. without issue.

    3. Hillegonda an Rensselaer, d. without issue.

    4. Eleanora Van Rensselaer, d. without issue.

    5. Susanna Van Rensselaer. M. Jan de la Court, and lived ana d. in Holland.

    6. Jan Baptist Van Rensselaer, first director of Rensselaerswyck; of whom below.

    7. *Jeremias Van Rensselaer*, third patroon and ancestor of the entire Van Rensselaer Family of America; of whom below.

    8. Rev. Nicolaus Van Rensselaer; of whom below.

    9. Ryckert Van Rensselaer, continued the Van Rensselaer line in Holland; of whom below.

    10. Wolter Van Rensselaer, d. without issue.

    11. Elizabeth Van Rensselaer. M. Johannes Van Rensselaer, of a branch of the family in Holland.

II

Kiliaen Van Rensselaer, the first patroon, died in the prime of life. Under the laws of Holland his children succeeded jointly in his estate, the headship of the eldest being recognized, but conferring no right to exclusive inheritance. For a number of years, however, the active management of the great colony in America was continued under a vice-director.

To this position Brandt Arendt Van Slichtenhorst was appointed in 1647, succeeding Van Corlaer. Like the Van Rensselaers, he was a native of Nykerk in Guelderland, and was a man of substance and character. His daughter, Margaretta, married Philip Pieterse Schuyler of Albany, founder of the Schuyler Family, and he is still represented by descendants among other prominent families of New York, including the Van Schaicks. In 1648 Van Slichtenhorst became involved in serious troubles with Governor Stuyvesant of New Netherland, resulting from the latter's contention that the land around Fort Orange belonged to the Dutch West India Company, and in general that he was entitled to exercise authority in the surrounding country regardless of the special privileges bestowed in the Van Rensselaer grant. This attitude of the governor was resisted by Van Slichtenhorst, whereupon Stuyvesant came up with a body of soldiers to enforce his demands. No actual passage at arms occurred, but the controversy raged with much bitterness for several years, and on one occasion Van Slichtenhorst was arrested and imprisoned by the governor's order. Years later it was legally determined that Stuyvesant's whole proceedings were without warrant, and that there could be no question of the sole proprietorship and sole jurisdiction of the Van Rensselaer Family.

Van Slichtenhorst continued in charge of Rensselaerswyck until superseded in 1652 by Jan Baptist Van Rensselaer, the second son of Kiliaen and the first of the family to assume personal direction of the colony.

It is noteworthy that under the government of the two vice-directors, Van Corlaer and Van Slichtenhorst, the patroonship rose to a flourishing condition, its prosperity even exceeding that of New Amsterdam. A very substantial foundation was laid for the future city of Albany, known in those times as Beverwyck. While none of the other Dutch colonies in America escaped Indian wars and ravages, Rensselaerswyck was throughout its history totally exempt from difficuties with the aborigines. Its good fortune in this respect was due to the prudent and just policy of Van Corlaer and Van Slichtenhorst, both of whom acquired much influence with the Five Nations; and the relations of amity thus established, being continued in after years by the Van Rensselaers and also by the responsible representatives of the provincial government in northern New York, afforded to the English colonies their main element of security and strength in their prolonged struggle for supremacy with the French.

JOHANNES VAN RENSSELAER, second patroon, was the eldest son of Kiliaen, and his only son by his first wife, Hillegonda Van Bylaer. He became head of the family at the death of his father, but never visited Rensselaerswyck. He died in early manhood.

Married Elizabeth Van Twiller.

Issue:

     1. Kiliaen Van Rensselaer, first lord of Van Rensselaer Manor; of whom below.

     2. Nella Van Rensselaer. M. Johan de Swardt.

JAN BAPTIST VAN RENSSELAER, second son of the first Kiliaen, and his first son by his second wife, Anna Van Wely, came to the colony of Rensselearswyck in 1651, accompanied by his youngest brother, Ryckert, then a child. He assumed the office of director on the 8th of May, 1652. During his residence on the estate he lived in a style befitting his position, having brought from Holland furniture, silverware, and other personal property of much value, with portraits of members of the Van Rensselaer Family. It was he who placed in the Dutch Church of Beverwyck in 1656 the window-pane representing the Van Rensselaer arms, quartered with those of its allied families. Not long afterward he returned to Holland, becoming one of the leading merchants of Amsterdam, where he died in 1678.

Married Susanna Van Wely.

Issue:

     1. Kiliaen Van Rensselaer, who remained in Holland and d. without issue.

JEREMIAS VAN RENSSELAER, third patroon, was the third son of the first Kiliaen, and his second son by his second wife, Anna Van Wely. He was born in Holland about 1632, received a superior education, and in 1658 came over to Rensselaerswyck to take the place of his brother Jan Baptist. He was the first of the family to establish himself permanently in America, the remainder of his life, sixteen years, being devoted to the government of the colony, which he exercised with great prudence, energy, and distinction. Pursuing the sagacious policy begun under the vice-directors, he became a man of great influence among the Indians, and "so attached them to him that they guarded his estates as carefully as they did their own." To the French in Canada he was known as one of the representative and ablest men of the Dutch and English colonies. He had the good judgment to adjust the acute differences with Stuyvesant which had so troubled the administrations of his brother and Van Slichtenhorst, and during the brief residue of the Dutch authority in New Netherland was on excellent terms with the irascible governor. On the occasion of the landtsdagh or diet summoned by Stuyvesant early in 1664 to deliberate on the critical condition of the province—this being the first general representative assembly held within the present state of New York,—he served as presiding officer of that body. After the surrender to the English in September of that year, he took the oath to the new government, and the rights and immunities enjoyed by his family in its colony of Rensselaerswyck were recognized, though the precise future status of the property was not settled in his time. He desired to obtain a new patent in the name of his family, and, failing in this, was privately advised to move in the matter as an individual (being qualified to hold real estate by virtue of his British citizenship), and so obtain a regrant of Rensselaerswyck in his personal name. This counsel he rejected indignantly, saying he was but a coheir, and would not defraud his brothers and sisters. He finally, however, obtained from Governor Andros a patent "to the heirs of Kiliaen Van Rensselaer," which, while in a sense only provisional, served all necessary purposes until the manor grant of 1685.

Jeremias left a voluminous correspondence, together with a minute chronicle of events in America, under the title of the "New Netherland Mercury." His great industry and methodical habits have been remarked upon by many writers. "His portrait," says Mrs. Lamb, "represents him as a remarkably handsome man of courtly presence," and his beautiful autograph is "one of the most characteristic that could be found in a century." (See Frontispiece.)

Died at Rensselaerswyck, October 12, 1674 (n. s.).

Married, July 12, 1662, Maria Van Cortlandt, daughter of Oloff Stevense and Annetje (Loockermans) Van Cortlandt, and sister of Stephanus Van Cortlandt, the founder of Van Cortlandt Manor. She was born in 1645 and died January 29, 1689.

Issue:

1. *Kiliaen Van Rensselaer,* second lord of Van Rensselaer Manor; see RENSSELAERSWYCK BRANCH, below.

2. Johannes Van Rensselaer, d. without issue.

3. Anna Van Rensselaer, b. in 1665. M., 1st, her first cousin, Kiliaen Van Rensselaer, first lord of the manor, son of Johannes and Elizabeth (Van Twiller) Van Rensselaer (above); m., 2d, William Nicoll.

4. *Hendrick Van Rensselaer,* who became proprietor of the "Eastern" Manor, comprising Greenbush and Claverack, and was the progenitor of the younger line of the Van Rensselaer Family; see GREENBUSH AND CLAVERACK BRANCH, below.

5. Maria Van Rensselaer. M. Peter Schuyler.

REV. NICOLAUS VAN RENSSELAER, fourth son of the first Kiliaen, and his third son by his second wife, Anna Van Wely, was born in Amsterdam, Holland, about 1638. He was liberally educated, taking his degree in theology. While on a tour of Europe he met the exiled King Charles II. at Brussels, and had the politeness to predict his speedy restoration to the British throne. A few years later, Charles being happily restored, Mr. Van Rensselaer went to England as chaplain of the Dutch embassy, and, being recognized by the sovereign, was presented by him with a gold snuff-box, which is still preserved among the heirlooms of the Van Rensselaer Family.

In England he took holy orders in the established church, and was appointed lecturer at St. Margaret's, Lothburg. In 1674 he came to America with a letter from the duke of York, who recommended that he be put in charge of one of the Dutch churches. This led to a heated theological contro- versy, an element of the Dutch Reformed organization re- garding Mr. Van Rensselaer as a divine of "papistical" tendencies. The antagonism went to such lengths that he was arrested and imprisoned "for some dubious words spoken in a sermon" at Albany, the complainants being the famous Jacob Leisler and Jacob Milburne. Compromises were effected, but his ministerial career was involved in vexations to the end.

He succeeded his brother Jeremias as head of Reusse- laerswyck, but enjoyed the position for only a brief time, dying at Albany in November, 1678.

Married, February 10, 1675, Alyda Schuyler, daughter of Philip Pieterse and Margaretta (Van Slichtenhorst) Schuyler; no issue. She remarried, in 1679, Robert Living- ston of Albany, later the grantee of Livingston Manor; and from them the elder line of the Livingston Family descends.

RYCKERT (RICHARD) VAN RENSSELAER, fifth son of the first Kiliaen, and his fourth son[2] by his second wife, Anna Van Wely, was born in Holland and came to America in 1651, with his brother Jan Baptist. He was for many years a magistrate of Albany, also having a part in the management of the colony after the death of Jeremias. He was the owner of the bouwerie called "The Flatts," four miles north of Albany, which he sold in 1670 to Philip

---

[2]According to a family tree now exisiting in Holland, he was the fourth son of the first Kiliaen, and his third son by his second wife, the Rev. Nico- laus being the youngest.

Pieterse Schuyler. Returning to Holland, he was for some time treasurer and burgomaster of Vianen in that country, and died about 1695.

Married, in Holland, Anna Van Beaumont, and had six sons and two daughters, of whom four sons and one daughter married.

His descendants continued the family name in Holland until 1815, when, upon the death of Jeremias Van Rensselaer, grandson of Ryckert's youngest son, Jeremias, the male line became extinct.

There was, however, an elder male descent through Ryckert's second son, Anthony Van Rensselaer, who married Bertha Pekstok. Their grandson, Jan Jacob Van Rensselaer, married Susanna Catherine Beeldsnyder, and died about the same time as his cousin Jeremias, leaving an only daughter, Sara Johanna Jacoba Van Rensselaer. She was the last of the Van Rensselaer surname in Holland; married Jonkheer Jan Van Bowier, and left twelve children. The late Vice-Admiral Marten Wilhelminus Van Rensselaer-Bowier of Amsterdam was her son and received by royal letters patent the right to bear his mother's name and arms in connection with his own and to transmit them to his legitimate descendants.

III

This generation, the third from Kiliaen the founder, witnessed the erection of the old patroonship of Rensselaerswyck into an English manor or lordship (1685, confirmed and more specifically brought under the provisions of the statute of primogenitureship in 1704). The hopes of the family were placed in Johannes's son Kiliaen, who became the first lord; but he died in 1687 without issue. After this mournful event the succession devolved on Jeremias's eldest son, Kiliaen; but he, though born in 1663, did not marry until 1701, and moreover his younger brother Hendrick, married in 1689, was for many years without male issue. Thus the continuance of the Van Rensselaer name and inheritance for a long time hung in uncertainty; but eventually heirs male were born to both the brothers. With them begin the two distinct lines of the Van Rensselaer Family which have come down to the present time; Kiliaen being the progenitor of the elder or Rensselaerswyck branch, and Hendrick of the younger or Greenbush and Claverack branch.

RENSSELAERSWYCK BRANCH

KILIAEN VAN RENSSELAER, first lord of the manor, the only son of Johannes and Elizabeth (Van Twiller) Van Rensselaer, was born in Holland, and, as the eldest male heir, received an education and rearing which corresponded to his station. Very little is known of his life, and indeed he is often confused by historical writers with his cousin and successor, Kiliaen, the son of Jeremias.

At the death of his uncle Jeremias in 1674 he was still in his minority, and until coming of age the estate of Rensselaerswyck was administered by his relatives; Rev. Nicolaus Van Rensselaer being director until his death (1678), Madame Maria Van Rensselaer (widow of Jeremias) acting as treasurer, and Stephanus Van Cortlandt (Madame Van Rensselaer's brother) serving in an advisory capacity.

The young Kiliaen received (in conjunction with his cousin Kiliaen, Jeremias's son) the manor grant of Rensselaerswyck, which was issued in the name of the duke of York by Governor Dongan on the 17th of October, 1685. In this instrument he was constituted the first lord of the manor.[3] Soon afterward occurred the first alienation of

_____

[3]The proprietors of Van Rensselaer Manor, as of the other manors of New York, are frequently alluded to by inexact writers—especially the authors of so-called historical novels—as "lords." Although it is true that the policy of the British colonial government was to encourage a semi-aristocratic society in America, and that tendency is well illustrated by the manor grants, the heads of the manorial families had no title or designation of gentility as such, and the term "lord of the manor" meant simply its owner or possessor. On this subject the present writer has said in a previous work: "The man-

Van Rensselaer lands—a tract running one mile along the river and sixteen miles west, which was relinquished to the government of the province of New York "for commons to the king," and this act of "magnanimous generosity of the Van Rensselaers" was followed, July 22, 1686, by the chartering of the city of Albany, embraced in the strip. It will be remembered that Stuyvesant had arbitrarily assumed to appropriate the lands about the old Fort Orange to the uses of the Dutch West India Company; but at the instance of the Van Rensselaer Family his action was legally reviewed by Governor Dongan, who reversed it, declaring that "The Town of Albany lyes within the Renslears colony. . . . They settled the place." The Van Rensselaers, however, rested content with the justice done in principle, and never attempted to resume possession of the property, although its value had greatly increased.

Kiliaen, the first lord, died in 1687, at Watervliet, N. Y.

Married Anna Van Rensselaer, daughter of Jeremias and Maria (Van Cortlandt) Van Rensselaer. No issue. His widow married, 2d, William Nicoll, by whom she had issue; from them come the Sill and Gardiner families—a present descendant being the wife of William Bayard Van Rensselaer, now head of the Van Rensselaer Family.

KILIAEN VAN RENSSELAER, second lord of the manor, the eldest son of Jeremias and Maria (Van Cortlandt) Van Rensselaer, was born on the Rensselaerswyck estate, August 24, 1663. He became the head of the family in 1687, upon the death of his cousin.

---

ors, one and all, were only ordinary landed estates granted to certain English subjects in America, who . . . enjoyed no distinguished rank whatever, and were in no way elevated titularly, by virtue of their manorial proprietorships, above the common people. In no case was a manorial grant . . . conferred upon a member of the British nobility, or even upon an individual boasting the minor rank of baronet; and in no case, moreover, was such a grant bestowed in recognition of services to the crown or as a mark of special honor by the sovereign. Without exception the proprietors of the manors were perfectly plain, untitled gentlemen."—See the able History of the Manors by the late Edward Floyd de Lancey in Scharf's "History of Westchester County."

Although his grandfather, the first Kiliaen, died in 1646, his estate had throughout all this time remained unsettled, being held in common, and apparently with good mutual understandings, by his various heirs. Besides the manor of Rensselaerswyck, the family possessions included much valuable property in Holland. It being desirable to effect a final division, Kiliaen of Rensselaerswyck, on his own behalf and that of his brothers and sisters (the American heirs), in 1695 entered into negotiations with Kiliaen of Amsterdam, son of Jan Baptist, who represented the heirs in the old country; and as the result the American lands were confirmed to the American heirs and the Holland lands to the Holland heirs. This arrangement was made conformably to Dutch usages. The ultimate disposal of the manorial property did not, however, depend on any such amicable family agreement, but was subject to the very precise English customs regarding inheritances of landed estates.

Agreeably to these customs, a new patent to the manor of Rensselaerswyck was issued by Queen Anne, May 20, 1704, which confirmed it to Kiliaen, and after him perpetually to his eldest male descent. Several days later, June 1, he released to his younger brother Hendrick the entire Claverack (Columbia County) Manor of sixty thousand acres, with some fifteen hundred acres of the upper manor, which included an island in the Hudson and the Greenbush or Crailo tract, one mile square. He also gave land to his sister, Mrs. Peter Schuyler, and his nephew, Rensselaer Nicoll.

He was one of the most prominent citizens of his times, being continuously in public life from 1691 to his death in 1719. The right to send a special deputy to the legislative assembly of New York was conferred upon Van Rensselaer Manor,[4] and in that body Kiliaen sat from its first session in 1691 until 1703. He was then elevated to the governor's

---

[4] The manor was continuously represented in the assembly throughout its colonial existence—1691 to 1775.

council, of which he was a member for the rest of his life, 1704 to 1719, and he also occupied the responsible position of commissioner of Indian affairs.

Died on the manor in 1719.

Married, October 15, 1701, Maria Van Cortlandt, daughter of Stephanus and Gertrude (Schuyler) Van Cortlandt. Issue:

1. Maria Van Rensselaer, b. 1702. M. Frederick Van Cortlandt.
2. Gertrude Van Rensselaer, b. 1703, d. 1704.
3. Jeremias Van Rensselaer, third lord of the manor; of whom below.
4. *Stephen Van Rensselaer I.*, fourth lord of the manor; of whom below.
5. Johannes Van Rensselaer, b. and d. 1711.
6. Gertrude Van Rensselaer, b. 1714. M. Adonis Schuyler of the New Jersey Schuyler Family.
7. John Baptist Van Rensselaer, b. 1717, d. unmarried, 1763.
8. Anna Van Rensselaer, b. 1719. M. John Schuyler of New Jersey.

IV

In this generation, as in the third, there were two lords of the manor. The first of these was

JEREMIAS VAN RENSSELAER, third lord, the eldest son of Kiliaen and Maria (Van Cortlandt) Van Rensselaer. He was born in 1705, represented the manor of Rensselaerswyck in the provincial assembly from 1726 to 1743, and was nominated and confirmed a member of the governor's council, but died, unmarried, soon afterward, in 1745, being succeeded by his brother,

STEPHEN VAN RENSSELAER I., fourth lord, the second son of Kiliaen and Maria (Van Cortlandt) Van Rensselaer. He was born on the manor, March 23, 1707. Being of quite delicate constitution, he took no part in public affairs, but for a time held the position of commissioner of Indian affairs. Died June, 1747.

Married, July 5, 1729, Elizabeth Groesbeck; she died December 31, 1756.

Issue:

    1. Kiliaen Van Rensselaer, b. 1730, d. young.

    2. Maria Van Rensselaer, b. 1731, d. 1734.

    3. Elizabeth Van Rensselaer, b. 1734. M., 1753, General Abraham Ten Broeck. He was many years a member of the provincial assembly (representing Van Rensselaer Manor); was colonel of militia, a member of the provincial congress of 1775, president of the state convention of 1776, brigadier-general in the Revolution, and later state senator of Albany, judge of the court of common pleas, and president of the Bank of Albany; d. January 19, 1810.

    4. Kiliaen Van Rensselaer, b. 1737, d. young.

    5. Maria Van Rensselaer, b. 1738, d. unmarried.

    6. *Stephen Van Rensselaer II.*, fifth lord of the manor; of whom below.

    7. Kiliaen Van Rensselaer, b. 1743, d. unmarried.

V

STEPHEN VAN RENSSELAER II., fifth lord of the manor, the eldest surviving son of Stephen and Elizabeth (Groesbeck) Van Rensselaer, was born on the manor, June 2, 1742. His father died when he was only five years old, and during his minority the affairs of the manor were administered by his brother-in-law, Colonel Abraham Ten Broeck, who also was its official representative in the assembly.

He is the best remembered in the family as the builder of the modern Manor House (1765).5 Like his father, his life was too brief to admit of any conspicuous participation in public concerns. In his time occurred the stamp act troubles and the division of popular sentiment in the colonies for and against the British crown. He was a vigorous opponent of the policy of the English government, and indeed all the Van Rensselaers of that period were staunch and aggressive American patriots.6

5The original Manor House, says the late Rev. Maunsell Van Rensselaer, was "a modest building of brick brought from Holland, by the side of the present Troy Road (which was not in existence then), opposite the present Manor House."

6There was no member of the manorial family old enough to bear arms during the early years of the Revolution, Stephen III., its next head, **not** coming of age until 1785, two years after the conclusion of peace. The

Died of a pulmonary disease, 1769, at the age of thirty-seven.

Married, January, 1764, Catharine Livingston, daughter of Philip Livingston, signer of the Declaration of Independence, and his wife, Christina Ten Broeck. Mrs. Van Rensselaer married, 2d, Rev. Eilardus Westerlo, by whom she left descendants.

Issue:

1. *Stephen Van Rensselaer III.,* sixth and last lord of the manor; of whom below.

2. Philip Schuyler Van Rensselaer, b. in Albany, April 15, 1767, and d. there, September 25, 1824. He was for nineteen years mayor of the city of Albany, was president of the Bank of Albany and the Albany Bible Society, a trustee of Union College, and one of the founders of the Albany Academy. M., 1787, Anne de Peyster Van Cortlandt, daughter of General Philip Van Cortlandt; no issue.

3. Elizabeth Van Rensselaer, b. 1768, d. 1841. M., 1st, September 18, 1787, John Bradstreet Schuyler, son of General Philip Schuyler; m., 2d, 1800, John Bleecker. By both marriages she left numerous descendants. A daughter, Catherine Westerlo Bleecker, m. Cornelius Glen Van Rensselaer of Greenbush, grandson of Colonel Johannes Van Rensselaer.

Claverack branch, however, had been quite productive of males. "At that momentous time," says Rev. Maunsell Van Rensselaer, "there were eighteen males of the Van Rensselaer name, of whom four, were boys and two were old men unable to endure military service. The remaining twelve all bore commissions in all the grades of the service."

Lieutenant-Governor Cadwallader Colden wrote to the earl of Dartmouth in 1775: "The present representatives of the manors [Rensselaerswyck and Claverack] have distinguished themselves in the opposition to government, and were the warmest supporters of the congress."

(To be continued.)

THE PHYSICAL EVOLUTION OF NEW YORK CITY IN A HUNDRED YEARS.

1807—1907.

BY JOHN AUSTIN STEVENS.

THE OLD CITY—THE NEW CITY.

First Paper.[1]

WHILE those interested in history and in the commemoration of important historic events are now looking forward to the tercenterary of the discovery of our great river by Hudson in 1609, and are eagerly engaged in preparations for a proper display of the wonderful outcome of that discovery, it is as well to recall the progress of development of our own city, which has made of it the greatest outlet of the product of the most prolific region of food supplies in the world—supplies without which the existence of the population of western Europe would be uncertain and hazardous. It is to be hoped that our great schemes of personal transportation by surface, elevated, and subway

[1]. It is proposed to treat this subject in two branches. The first, a picture of the old city, is arranged from the address before the New York Historical Society in November, 1900, "New York in the Nineteenth Century," which was the basis of the papers on this theme printed last year in this Magazine. The second, a picture of the new city on the lines laid down in the commissioners' plan of 1807, and the evolution in the century ending 1907, must, of course, be delayed until the statistics of the beginning of that year are made public.

The commissioners were allowed four years in which to complete their plan, and it was not till 1811 that their report, with an accompanying map, was filed. There is a copy of this map in the New York Historical Society. The Embargo Act utterly paralyzed all business in 1807 and stopped all physical development of the city of New York. There could hardly have been any changes in the face of the city from the date of the creation of the commission and the filing of its report.

S. Van Rensselaer

THE VAN RENSSELAER FAMILY.

BY W. W. SPOONER.

(Continued.)

VI

STEPHEN VAN RENSSELAER III, sixth and last lord of the manor, the eldest son of Stephen and Catharine (Livingston) Van Rensselaer, was born in New York City, November 1, 1764. He was graduated from Harvard College in 1782, and, assuming the direction of his great estate, adopted a policy of energetic development of its lands. He placed the rentals so low that they yielded only one per cent. on a fair valuation, and in consequence soon had under cultivation some nine hundred farms of one hundred and fifty acres each, a number which was greatly increased later.

In 1789 he entered political life as a member of the assembly. He served in the state senate from 1791 to 1796, was elected lieutenant-governor in 1795 and 1798, was a candidate for governor in 1801, and was again in the assembly from 1808 to 1810. One of the first to advocate the construction of a canal between the Hudson River and the Great Lakes, he was appointed in 1810 a commissioner to report regarding the route, made a tour of investigation, and signed the favorable report on that subject submitted to the legislature in 1811. Owing, however, to the breaking out of the war with England, the enterprise was suspended for some years.

Previously to this conflict he was of the conservative party, which opposed hostilities, but he was prompt to offer

(129)

his services to the government. His connection with military affairs began in 1786, when he was made a major of infantry in the New York militia. Two years later he was promoted to a colonelcy, and in 1801 became major-general of cavalry. Retaining the latter rank he was appointed in 1812 to command the United States forces on the Canadian frontier, instituted a strong organization of the militia, and on October 13 fought the brilliant battle of Queenstown Heights, in which the British general, Brock, was killed, the American advance being led by General Van Rensselaer's kinsman, Lieutenant-Colonel Solomon Van Rensselaer,[7] who was severely wounded in the attack. All the advantage of the victory was, however, lost by the refusal of the militia to move across the river and support the successful party on the Heights, which was obliged to surrender, and the whole expedition thus resulted in failure. Voluntarily resigning his command soon afterward, the general took no further part in the war.

Upon the restoration of peace the Erie Canal project was resumed, and General Van Rensselaer again became commissioner. With this great enterprise he was identified to its successful completion, and indeed continued on the board for the rest of his life, serving as its president for many years. He was once more elected a member of the assembly in 1818, was a member of the constitutional convention of 1821, and represented his district in congress from 1823 to 1829. He occupied various other positions of prominence and dignity, including those of regent and chancellor of the New York State University, and president of the State Agricultural Society, and was the first president of the Albany Savings Bank, which was incorporated in 1820 and is now the second oldest savings institution in the state.

General Van Rensselaer's name is perpetuated by the Rensselaer Polytechnic Institute of Troy, the first institu-

---

7A son of Henry Kiliaen Van Rensselaer of the Claverack branch, and great-grandson of Hendrick Van Rensselaer.

tion of its special character established in the country. It was founded by him in 1824, with suitable buildings and equipment and a liberal endowment, as "a school to qualify teachers to instruct the application of experimental chemistry, philosophy, and natural history to agriculture, domestic economy, and to the arts and manufactures." For some fourteen years he sustained it at his own expense. He received from Yale in 1825 the degree of LL.D.

The general was the last of the family to retain in its entirety the estate of Rensselaerswyck. The liberal and enterprising policy as its proprietor which he adopted in early manhood he pursued consistently throughout life, and and as the result the population of the manor increased immensely. But, clinging to the traditions of his race, he uniformly refused to sell lands, and thus the inhabitants of a territory covering the larger part of two great counties still occupied the ancient position of tenants of a single landlord. Moreover, all the old-time conditions and customs attaching to the tenantship were preserved in full vigor. Rents were paid not in money but in produce, the annual rates ranging from ten bushels of wheat per hundred acres in the townships earlier settled to fourteen in those of later settlement; with the addition for all farms alike of four fat hens and one day's service to the landlord with horses and wagon. "Residents of Albany," said a writer in 1887, "still remember seeing the road in the vicinity of the Manor House blocked up with long lines of wagons in from the country with wheat and chickens to pay their rent, or with loads of wood, which were generally accepted in lieu of one day's labor required." Another old usage which was retained without modification was the requirement that if any tenant disposed of his leasehold to a third party he should pay the landlord either one-fourth the amount received (whence the term "quarter-sales"), or one additional year's rent.

These various conditions and customs, though well suited

to a primitive age, in time came to be regarded by the tenantry with distaste, and though during the life of General Van Rensselaer no active dissatisfaction was manifested, it needed no penetration to see that a change was impending. Curiously enough, the agitation against the rent system which burst forth after his death resulted primarily from the policy of exceptional generosity and leniency to his tenants which he had uniformly practiced. One of the kindliest and most liberal of men, he never evicted delinquent debtors, and never forced or urged payments of the rental, even when long in arrears. Thus he permitted indebtedness to accumulate and multiply, which at his death aggregated the enormous total of $400,000. In his will, with his characteristic generosity, he provided expressly that the discharge of debts owing by persons in circumstances of poverty, misfortune, or inability should not be insisted on; but he did not think it just to his heirs, or right in any point of view, to remit lawful debts incurred to his estate through his magnanimous indulgence, especially as that estate was burdened with very heavy pecuniary obligations. He stipulated, consequently, that the debts due to him should be applied to liquidating his debts to others.

At his death the tenants, anxious about their debts and seeing these had not been remitted, were quick to apprehend that measures for settlement would follow. From this apprehension sprang the whole "Anti-Rent" propaganda, which soon assumed such formidable proportions.

The Van Rensselaer Manor was devised by the general to his two eldest sons, Stephen and William P., the former receiving the portion on the west side of the Hudson, and the latter that on the east side. The following figures (for the year 1846) indicate the extent of cultivation of the estate as left by him, with the annual revenues: Albany County—1,397 leasehold farms, covering 233,900 acres, and yielding an annual rent of 23,390 bushels of wheat; Rensselaer County—1,666 leasehold farms, having a total of 202,-

100 acres, and charged yearly with 20,210 bushels of wheat. Among his other children General Van Rensselaer divided his remaining real estate and various personal property, including lands in Saratoga and Hamilton counties, land and houses in Albany and New York City, and stocks of different kinds.

Died at the Manor House, January 26, 1839. In the public events which ensued he was always referred to as the "Old Patroon," his eldest son and principal successor, Stephen IV., being styled the "Young Patroon."

Married, 1st, 1783, Margarita Schuyler, daughter of General Philip and Catherine (Van Rensselaer) Schuyler; she was born in 1758, died 1801.

Issue:

1. Catharine Schuyler Van Rensselaer, b. 1784, d. 1787.
2. Stephen Van Rensselaer, b. 1786, d. 1787.
3. *Stephen Van Rensselaer IV.; of whom below.*

General Stephen Van Rensselaer married, 2d, May 17, 1802, Cornelia Paterson, daughter of Hon. William Paterson, justice of the United States supreme court, and his wife, Cornelia Bell. The second Mrs. Van Rensselaer was born 1780 and died 1844.

Issue:

4. Catharine Van Rensselaer, b. 1803. M., June 2, 1830, Gouverneur Morris Wilkins; no issue.

5. William Paterson Van Rensselaer, b. 1805, d. in New York City, November 13, 1872. Graduated from Yale College in 1824, he spent the next four years in foreign travel, and for some time pursued further studies in Scotland and Germany. He received from his father the Rensselaer County lands of the manor, which he eventually sold. For the last twenty years of his life he resided at Rye, Westchester County, N. Y. Possessed of an ample fortune, he was noted for his practical benevolences, which, however, were exercised with avoidance of all display. He was zealous and active in the church, and his private character was most exemplary. M., 1st, May 13, 1833, Eliza Rogers, daughter of Benjamin Woolsey Rogers. Issue: i. William Paterson Van Rensselaer, b. 1835, d. 1854. ii. Susan Bayard Van Rensselaer, b. 1840, d. 1863.—Mr. Van Rensselaer m., 2d, April 4, 1839, Sarah Rogers, a sister of his

first wife. Issue: iii. Cornelia Paterson Van Rensselaer, m., April 22, 1862, John Erving. iv. Walter S. Van Rensselaer, b. 1843, d. 1865. v. Kiliaen Van Rensselaer of New York City, b. 1845, d. 1905; was a soldier in the Civil War; a member of the Loyal Legion, the Holland, St. Nicholas, and Huguenot societies, and other organizations; prominent in religious and philanthropic work; m., December 13, 1870, Olivia Atterbury, a descendant of the famous Bishop Atterbury of England and a granddaughter of Anson G. Phelps. vi. Sarah E. Van Rensselaer, b. 1847, d. 1869. vii. Arthur Van Rensselaer, b. 1848, d. 1859. viii. Catherine G. Van Rensselaer, m., June 11, 1891, Anson Phelps Atterbury. ix. Eleanor Van Rensselaer, m., June 1, 1887, Hamilton K. Fairfax.

Eighth Generation from Kiliaen the founder.—Issue of Cornelia Paterson Van Rensselaer and John Erving: i. Susan Erving. ii. Cornelia Van Rensselaer Erving, m., June 11, 1895, John V. L. Pruyn (he d. 1904). iii. J. Langdon Erving. iv. Emily Elwyn Erving, m., January 22, 1895, Henry Woodward Cooper. v. Sarah E. Erving, m., April 22, 1896, James Gore King. vi. William Van Rensselaer Erving. vii. Katharine Erving. viii. Eleanor Erving. ix. Shirley Erving. x. Justine Bayard Erving.—Issue of Kiliaen Van Rensselaer and Olivia Atterbury: i. Olive Atterbury Van Rensselaer. ii. Sarah Elizabeth Van Rensselaer, m. Benjamin Walworth Arnold. iii. Katharine Boudinot Van Rensselaer, d. 1897. iv. Kiliaen Van Rensselaer, m., 1905, Dorothy Manson. v. William Stephen Van Rensselaer.—Issue of Eleanor Van Rensselaer and Hamilton R. Fairfax: i. Katharine Van Rensselaer Fairfax. ii. Hamilton Fairfax.

Ninth Generation from Kiliaen the founder.—Issue of Cornelia Van Rensselaer Erving and John V. L. Pruyn: i. Erving Pruyn.—Issue of Emily Elwyn Erving and Henry Woodward Cooper: i. Cornelia Van Rensselaer Cooper.—Issue of Sarah E. Erving and James Gore King: i. James Gore King. ii. Eleanor Erving King. iii. Edward Ramsay King.

6. Philip Van Rensselaer, b. 1806, d. 1871. M., October 17, 1839, Mary R. Tallmadge, daughter of General James Tallmadge; she was b. 1817, d. 1872. Issue:

i. James Tallmadge Van Rensselaer of Fairfield, Conn. M., 1897, Mrs. Minnie (Sackett) Parker.

ii. Philip Van Rensselaer, d. March 22, 1882. M., September 8, 1872, Edith Biddle.

7. *Rev. Cortlandt Van Rensselaer, D. D.;* of whom below.

8. Henry Bell Van Rensselaer, b. 1810, d. March 23, 1864. He was graduated from West Point in 1831, but resigned from the army and engaged in farming near Ogdensburg, N. Y. From his

father he inherited lands in Saratoga County. In 1841-3 he was a member of congress; later he was connected with mining enterprises. At the beginning of the Civil War he returned to the army, being appointed chief of staff to General Winfield Scott, with the rank of brigadier-general. "He became inspector-general with the rank of colonel on the retirement of General Scott, served in the department of the Rappahannock in April and August, 1862, subsequently in the Third Army Corps, and in the department of the Ohio from September 17 until his death." M., August 22, 1833, Elizabeth Ray King, daughter of Governor John Alsop and Mary (Ray) King. Issue: i. Mary Van Rensselaer, m., April 28, 1874, John Henry Screven. ii. Cornelia Van Rensselaer, m., April 26, 1859, James L. Kennedy. iii. Stephen Van Rensselaer of New York City, b. October 29, 1836, d. January 20, 1904; captain in the United States army; a member of the Union Club, St. Nicholas Society, and other organizations; m., December 9, 1869, Mathilda C. Heckscher, daughter of Charles Heckscher. iv. Henry Van Rensselaer, d. young. v. Euphemia Van Rensselaer (Sister Marie Dolores). vi. Elizabeth Van Rensselaer, m., June 3, 1873, George Waddington. vii. John King Van Rensselaer of New York City, b. at Ogdensburg, N. Y., July 17, 1847; president of the Stirling Fire Insurance Company; m., October 24, 1871, May Denning King, daughter of Archibald Gracie King. viii. Katharine Van Rensselaer, m., January 17, 1870, Dr. Francis Delafield. ix. Rev. Henry Van Rensselaer, S. J. x. Westerlo Van Rensselaer, d. young.

Eighth Generation from Kiliaen the founder.—Issue of Mary Van Rensselaer and John Henry Screven: i. Elizabeth Ray Screven, m., January 5, 1897, Ernest E. Lorillard.—Issue of Cornelia Van Rensselaer and James L. Kennedy: i. H. Van Rensselaer Kennedy, m., March 4, 1886, Marion Robbins. —Issue of Captain Stephen Van Rensselaer and Mathilda C. Heckscher: i. Charles A. Van Rensselaer, merchant in New York City; m., December 12, 1899, Caroline E. Fitz Gerald, daughter of Desmond and Elizabeth (Salisbury) Fitz Gerald of Brookline, Mass. ii. Elizabeth Van Rensselaer, m., February 27, 1900, John Magee Ellsworth. iii. Stephen Van Rensselaer, m. Marion W. Farlin. iv. Mathilde Van Rensselaer.— Issue of Elizabeth Van Rensselaer and George Waddington: i. Mary E. Waddington. ii. Euphemia Waddington, m. Christopher B. Wyatt of New York.—Issue of John King Van Rensselaer, b. July 5, 1872; resides in New York City; m., January 30, 1896, Helen F. Galindo. ii. Frederick Harold Van Rensselaer, b. January 6, 1874, d. August 6, 1903; m., April 23, 1898, Josephine Lucy Grinnell, daughter of Robert Minturn and Sophie (Van Alen) Grinnell.—Issue of Katharine Van Rens-

selaer and Dr. Francis Delafield: i. Elizabeth Ray Delafied. ii.
Julia Floyd Delafield, m., November 11, 1896, Frederick S.
Crosby. iii. Cornelia Van Rensselaer Delafield. iv. Edward
Ninth Generation from Kiliaen the founder.—Issue of
H. Van Rensselaer Kennedy and Marion Robbins: i.
Rachel Kennedy. ii. Marion Kennedy. iii. Maud Ken-
nedy.—Issue of Charles A. Van Rensselaer and Caroline
E. Fitz Gerald: i. Charles A. Van Rensselaer, Jr., b.
September 29, 1902. ii. Stephen Van Rensselaer, b. No-
vember 28, 1905.—Issue of Elizabeth Van Rensselaer and
John Magee Ellsworth: i. Elizabeth Van Rensselaer
Ellsworth. ii. Matilda Coster Ellsworth. iii. Stephen Van
Rensselaer Ellsworth.—Issue of Frederick Harold Van
Rensselaer and Josephine Lucy Grinnell: i. L. Sylvia Grin-
nell Van Rensselaer.—Issue of Julia F. Delafield and Fred-
eric S. Crosby: i. Katharine Van Rensselaer Crosby.

9. Cornelia Paterson Van Rensselaer, b. 1812. M., February
16, 1847, Robert J. Turnbull, M. D. Issue: i. Katharine Euphemia
Turnbull.

10. Alexander Van Rensselaer, b. 1814, d. May 8, 1878. M.,
1st, October 21, 1851, Mary Howland, daughter of S. S. Howland;
2d, June 30, 1864, Louisa Barnewall, daughter of William and Cle-
mentina (Rutgers) Barnewall. Issue (by second marriage):
i. Louisa Van Rensselaer. M., June 18, 1887, Edmund L.
Baylies.
ii. Mabel Van Rensselaer. M., M. V. R. Johnson.
iii. Alice Van Rensselaer.

11. Euphemia White Van Rensselaer, b. 1816, d. 1888. M.,
May 2, 1843, John Church Cruger. Issue:
i. Stephen Van Rensselaer Cruger, b. 1844, d. June 23,
1898. M., April 21, 1868, Jullie G. Storrow.
ii. Cornelia Cruger.
iii. Catharine Cruger.

VII

STEPHEN VAN RENSSELAER IV., eldest surviving
son of General Stephen Van Rensselaer (by his first wife,
Margarita Schuyler), was born on the manor, March 29,
1789. He was graduated from Princeton College in 1808, and
in 1839, at the age of fifty, inherited from his father all of
the manor lying in Albany County. He made great
improvements in the Manor House, which indeed he caused
to be largely reconstructed (from designs by Upjohn) and
entirely refitted. Soon after his father's death began the

"Anti-Rent" agitation on his property, which in its origin, as seen above, was mainly due to the unwillingness of his delinquent debtors to discharge their arrearages. It soon assumed the character of an economic and political movement against the whole system of leasehold land tenures, special stress being laid by the agitators upon the burdensomeness, as claimed, of the "quarter-sales" provisions. Efforts at compromise failed, and the movement, prosecuted with great acrimony and attended by serious disturbances and even bloodshed, continued for several years. The questions involved were finally settled legally by amendments to the constitution of 1846, which abolished both the leasehold tenures and the quarter-sales. The lands of the manor were sold by the proprietor at great sacrific.

To the end of his life he continued to reside in the Manor House, in the enjoyment of an estate which, while no longer of vast territorial extent, was of most solid character and highly productive. He occupied the position of major-general of militia. Personally he was a man of high attainments, and was much beloved. He was known as the "Young Patroon" and sometimes the "last of the patroons."

Died May 25, 1868.

Married, January 31, 1817, Harriet Elizabeth Bayard, daughter of William Bayard of New York City; she was born in 1799 and died in 1875 at the Manor House.

Issue:

1. Margaret S. Van Rensselaer, b. 1819, d. September 5, 1897. M., 1st, 1837, John de P. Douw. Issue: i. Henry A. Douw. ii. Harriet Van Rensselaer Douw, b. 1842, d. 1862.—Mrs. Margaret S. (Van Rensselaer) Douw m., 2d, 1851, Wilmot Johnson.

2. Cornelia P. Van Rensselaer, b. 1823, d. May, 1897. M., June 10, 1846, Nathaniel Thayer. Issue:

i. Stephen Van Rensselaer Thayer, b. 1847, d. October, 1871. M., November 2, 1870, Alice Robeson, daughter of Andrew Robeson. Issue: 1. Stephen Van Rensselaer Thayer, m., June 5, 1895, Julia Porter, daughter of Augustus Porter (their children being Alice Thayer, Julia Porter Thayer, and Mary Allen Thayer).

ii. Cornelia Van Rensselaer Thayer. M., November 24,

1868, J. Hampden Robb. Issue: 1. N. Thayer Robb, m., November 25, 1895, Beatrix Henderson, daughter of Charles R. Henderson (their children being Janet Henderson Robb, James Hampden Robb, and Cornelia Van Rensselaer Robb). 2. Cornelia Van Rensselaer Robb. 3. Louisa Robb, m., April 8, 1896, Goodhue Livingston (their children being Goodhue Livingston, Jr., and Cornelia Thayer Livingston). 4. Harriet Bayard Robb.

iii. Nathaniel Thayer. M., 1st, February 1, 1881, Cornelia C. Barroll. Issue: 1. Cornelia Van Rensselaer Thayer. 2. Anna Morton Thayer, m., 1904, William Patton (two children). 3. Sarah Barroll Thayer.—Nathaniel Thayer m., 2d, June 11, 1887, Pauline Revere.

iv. Harriet Bayard Thayer, b. 1853, d. 1891. M., October 11, 1883, J. Forrester Andrew. Issue: 1. Cornelia Thayer Andrew, m., 1904, Dudley Clark of Boston (two children). 2. Elizabeth Andrew, m., 1905, Charles Ellis Mason.

v. Eugene Van Rensselaer Thayer. M., 1880, Susan Spring. Issue: 1. Eugene Van Rensselaer Thayer, Jr., m. Gladys Brooks. 2. Katharine Thayer, m. Howland Russell (one child). 3. Susan Thayer.

vi. John E. Thayer, b. 1862. M., 1886, Evelyn Forbes. Issue: 1. John E. Thayer. 2. Evelyn Thayer. 3. Nora Thayer. 4. Nathalie Thayer.

vii. Bayard Thayer. M., September 1, 1896, Ruth Simpkins. Issue: 1. Ruth Thayer. 2. Nathaniel Thayer. 3. Constance Thayer.

3. Stephen Van Rensselaer, b. 1824, d. 1861. M., August 20, 1858, Annie Louise Wild; no issue.

4. Catharine Van Rensselaer, b. 1826. M., October 14, 1856, Nathaniel Berry. Issue: i. Catharine Van Rensselaer Berry. ii. Walter Van Rensselaer Berry. iii. Nathalie Berry.

5. Justine Van Rensselaer, b. 1828. M., February, 1853, Howard Townsend. Issue:

i. Justine Van Rensselaer Townsend, b. 1853, d. 1881. M., June 23, 1877, Thomas H. Barber of the United States army.

ii. Howard Townsend, b. August 23, 1858. M., 1st, April 17, 1888, Sophie Dickey. Issue: 1. Sophie Townsend. 2. Howard Townsend, d. young.—Howard Townsend m., 2d, October, 1894, Anne Lowndes Langdon. Issue: 3. Anne Langdon Townsend. 4. Howard Van Rensselaer Townsend. 5. Eugene Langdon Townsend. 6. Philip Schuyler Townsend.

iii. Stephen Van Rensselaer Townsend, b. October, 1860, d. January 15, 1901. M., May 22, 1888, Janet Eckford King, daughter of Cornelius L. King. Issue: 1. Janet King Townsend. 2. Margaret Schuyler Townsend. 3. Stephen Van Rensselaer Townsend. 4. Justine Van Rensselaer Townsend.

iv. Harriet Bayard Townsend. M., April 28, 1886, Thomas H. Barber of the United States army. Issue: 1. Thomas H. Barber. 2. Justine Van Rensselaer Barber.

6. *Bayard Van Rensselaer;* of whom below.

7. Harriet Van Rensselaer. M., 1863, J. Schuyler Crosby. Issue:

i. Stephen Van Rensselaer Crosby. M., September 18, 1895, Henrietta Marion Grew, daughter of Henry Sturgis Grew. Issue: 1. Henry Grew Crosby. 2. Katharine Crosby.

ii. Angelica Schuyler Crosby. M., 1903, John B. Henderson. Issue, a daughter, b. July 5, 1906.

8. Eugene Van Rensselaer, b. October 12, 1840. M., 1865, Sally K. Pendleton. Issue:

i. Elizabeth K. Van Rensselaer.

ii. Rev. Stephen Van Rensselaer, resides in Monticello, N. Y. M., October 10, 1900, Mary Thorn Carpenter, who d. October, 1902.

REV. CORTLANDT VAN RENSSELAER, D. D., seventh child and fourth surviving son of Stephen Van Rensselaer III. (his mother being the latter's second wife, Cornelia Paterson), was born at the Manor House, May 26, 1808. He was graduated from Yale in 1827, and then studied law, being admitted to the bar of New York in 1830. Concluding, however, to engage in the ministry, he pursued the necessary studies to that end at the Union Theological Seminary of Prince Edward County, Va., and the Princeton Theological Seminary. He was ordained in the Presbyterian ministry in 1833. During the next two years he devoted himself very earnestly to missionary labors among the slaves in Virginia. He was installed pastor of the First Presbyterian Church of Burlington, N. J., in 1837, but resigned that charge three years later.

For the next two or three years he resided in Washington, D. C., having pastoral charge of the Second Presbyterian Church of that city. In 1843 he accepted an invitation from the board of directors of the Princeton Theological Seminary to undertake an agency for increasing the endowment of the institution. In starting upon this work he made a personal contribution of $2,000 to the fund.

The results of his efforts exceeded all expectations, the sum of $100,000 being raised.

From 1847 until his death he occupied the important posi- of corresponding secretary and principal executive officer of the Presbyterian board of education. Introducing new and enlightened methods in the administration of this office, he greatly extended the scope of the educational work of the church, also founding and editing the *Presbyterian Magazine* and *The Home, the School, and Church.*

He received the degree of doctor of divinity from the University of New York in 1845.

Dr. Van Rensselaer was one of the most conspicuous figures of his times in the Presbyterian Church, and is remembered especially for the great practical usefulness of his labors in its behalf. His life was distinguished by ceaseless energy, zeal, and the sincerest piety. During his last illness he received the unexampled compliment of a message of affectionate condolence from the general assembly (then in session), signed by all its officers and members. He made it a uniform rule to donate to charity whatever money he received for his services, and in addition was a very liberal giver from his private means. Selections from his writings were published in 1861, under the title of "Miscellaneous Sermons, Essays, and Addresses." These include his notable "Historical Discourse on the Occasion of the Centennial Celebration of the Battle of Lake George," many funeral orations, and papers on theological and educational subjects.

Died at Burlington, N. J., July 25, 1860.

Married, September 13, 1836, Catherine Ledyard Cogswell, daughter of Dr. Mason Fitch and Mary Austin (Ledyard) Cogswell of Connecticut. She was born September 22, 1811, at Hartford, Conn.; died September 13, 1836. Her father (a graduate of Yale, 1780) was a descendant of the Cogswell Family which came from Wilts County, England; and on the side of his mother (Alice Fitch) traced his ancestry to the distinguished Fitch Family of Connecticut and also to the famous Captain John Mason. Mrs. Van Rensselaer's mother, Mary Austin (Ledyard) Cogswell, was a daughter of John Ledyard, who came from England in 1700, and was collaterally related to Colonel William Ledyard, the hero of Fort Griswold.

Issue:

1. Cortlandt Van Rensselaer, b. January 5, 1838. He was a captain in the Thirteenth Infantry, United States army, and served with credit and distinction in the Civil War. D. at Nashville, Tenn., October 7, 1864, from the effects of wounds received at the battle of Mission Ridge.

2. Philip Livingston Van Rensselaer, b. November 24, 1839; was a major in the Second New Jersey Cavalry; d. at Vevey, Switzerland, March 10, 1873. M. Anne Whitmore of Boston, Mass.; no issue.

3. Charles Chauncey Van Rensselaer, b. January 16, 1842, d. May 17, 1843.

4. Ledyard Van Rensselaer, b. November 20, 1843; was a physician at Burlington, N. J.; d. March 26, 1893.

5. Alice Cogswell Van Rensselaer, b. March 19, 1846, d. April 18, 1878. M., May 7, 1868, Rev. Edward B. Hodge, son of Hugh L. Hodge, M.D., LL.D., and Margaret E. (Aspinwall) Hodge. He was b. February 5, 1841, d. June 15, 1906; was graduated from the University of Pennsylvania in 1859 and the Princeton Theological Seminary in 1863; was pastor of the Presbyterian Church of Burlington, N. J., from 1864 to 1893; was corresponding secretary of the Presbyterian board of education and trustee and director of the Princeton Theological Seminary; received the degree of D.D. from Princeton in 1893; resided in Philadelphia. Issue: i. Margaret Hodge. ii. Cortlandt Van Rensselaer Hodge, killed in China during the "Boxer" troubles, while serving in that country as a medical missionary of the Presbyterian Church; m. Elsie Sinclair of Philadelphia. iii. Edward B. Hodge, Jr.; m. Gretchen Green. iv. Catharine Hodge.

6. Elizabeth Wadsworth Van Rensselaer, b. February 22, 1848, d. April 17, 1886. M., October 6, 1868, General Edward Burd Grubb of New Jersey. He was b. at Burlington, N. J., November 13, 1841, son of Edward Burd Grubb, Sr., and is descended from a family of large landed estate, derived by patent from William Penn. He was graduated with honors from Burlington College in 1860; served with distinction in the Civil War, rising through various grades to the rank of brigadier-general. General Grubb is one of the most prominent and honored citizens of New

Jersey. He was the republican candidate for governor in 1888, and the following year was appointed by President Harrison United States minister to Spain. In that capacity he performed valuable services, among these being the negotiation of a reciprocity treaty with the Spanish government. Issue: i. Euphemia Van Rensselaer Grubb, m., November 20, 1895, Charles D. Halsey, their children being: 1. Van Rensselaer Halsey. 2. Charles Day Halsey.

7. Alexander Van Rensselaer, b. October 1, 1850. He was graduated from Princeton in the class of 1871; is a well-known citizen of Philadelphia. M., January 27, 1898, Mrs. Sarah (Drexel) Fell, widow of John Fell and daughter of Anthony Joseph and Ellen (Rozet) Drexel of Philadelphia.

VIII

BAYARD VAN RENSSELAER, second son of Stephen Van Rensselaer IV. and Harriet Elizabeth (Bayard) Van Rensselaer, was born in Albany, September 8, 1833. He was educated at Churchill's Military Academy at Sing Sing, N. Y.

Died at Pau, France, at the early age of twenty-five, January 12, 1859.

Married, 1854, Laura Reynolds, youngest daughter of Marcus T. Reynolds, a prominent lawyer of Albany.

Issue:

1. *William Bayard Van Rensselaer;* of whom below.

2. Howard Van Rensselaer, b. June 26, 1858. He received his early education at the Albany Normal School and St. Paul's School, Concord, N. H., and was graduated at Yale as bachelor of philosophy in 1881 and at the New York College of Physicians and Surgeons as doctor of medicine in 1884. After eighteen months of service as interne in the New York Hospital he went abroad and for two years (1887-9) pursued further studies in the leading European hospitals. Returning to Albany, he became prominent in his profession and actively identified with the local hospitals, as well as with the Albany Medical College, in which he has long been a prominent member of the teaching staff. Dr. Van Reusselaer is widely known as a writer on medical and sanitary subjects, and is editor of the *Albany Medical Annals.*

IX

WILLIAM BAYARD VAN RENSSELAER, eldest son

of Bayard and Laura (Reynolds) Van Rensselaer, is now the head of the Van Rensselaer Family, and if the entail had continued would be the eighth lord of the manor. In his residence are preserved a large portion of the woodwork and some of the furniture of the Van Rensselaer Manor House. He was born in Albany, October 4, 1856, was graduated from Harvard in 1879, and then studeid law one year at the Harvard Law School and afterward in the office of Marcus T. Hun, a noted jurist in Albany. After his admission to the bar, in 1881, he practiced his profession for a time, but discontinued it to take up the management of the Van Rensselaer estate.

He has since been prominently identified with business and financial interests in Albany. In 1900 he was elected president of the Albany Savings Bank, the largest financial institution in that city, of which his great-grandfather, Stephen Van Rensselaer III., was the first president (1820-39). He is also president of the Savings Bank Association of New York State, president of the Albany Terminal Warehouse Company, vice-president of the New York State National Bank, and vice-president of the Union Trust Company of Albany. He is one of the executive committee of the New York State Normal College at Albany and a member of the chapter of All Saints' (Episcopalian) Cathedral.

Married, November 3, 1880, Louisa Greenough Lane, daughter of Professor George M. Lane, for many years head of the classical department in Harvard University, and Frances Gardiner.

(To be continued.)

GEORGE WASHINGTON'S FIRST EXPERIENCE AS A SURVEYOR.

BY WALTER BUELL.

WASHINGTON'S early education was in the direction to fit him in an especial manner for the practical work of a surveyor. After having exhausted the possibilities of the elementary school, which he had before attended, he was taken into the family of his brother Lawrence, that he might have the benefit of a better one than existed in that neighborhood. It seems to have been intended that he should attain a thorough and practical business education—such as should fit him for all the duties of an extensive colonial land owner and planter. Perhaps the possibility of his becoming a magistrate or burgess was also present, as the place that awaited him in the society of Virginia was such as to warrant so modest an ambition. There are now in existence several of his school-books, into one of which are copied, with infinite pains, forms for contracts, land conveyances, leases, mortgages, etc. In another are preserved the field-notes and calculations of surveys, which he made as a matter of practice—kept and proved with the same exactness that would have been expected had the result been intended to form the basis of practical transactions. Not the least advantage of Washington's sojourn with his brother was the fact that it introduced him, at once, into the highest and, at the same time, the best society of the colony. Lawrence had become one of the most honored and prominent men in Virginia. His wealth, his social position and that of the Fairfax family, his sterling character and unquestioned ability, had united to advance him,

(144)

Fort Crailo—The Van Rensselaer Mansion, 1663

THE VAN RENSSELAER FAMILY.

BY W. W. SPOONER.

(Concluded.)

Greenbush and Claverack Branch.

AS has been seen under III. heretofore, the Van Rensselaer Family in its third American generation divided into two distinct lines—first, the so-called ''Rensselaerswyck'' line, from Kiliaen, eldest son of Jeremias and Maria (Van Cortlandt) Van Rensselaer, and second, the ''Greenbush and Claverack'' line, from Hendrick, youngest son of the same; these brothers being the only American male grandchildren of the first Kiliaen of Amsterdam by whom the surname was continued.

Throughout colonial times and until the death of General Stephen Van Rensselaer (1839), the Rensselaerswyck family, preserving its vast estate as a hereditary unit under the system of entail, occupied a greatly preponderating position in the respect of magnitude and concentration of possessions; and well corresponding to the prestige by which it was thus distinguished was its reputation for character and worth represented by its successive heads. But during the period stated this elder branch was numerically small; from Kiliaen, of the third generation, to General Stephen, of the sixth, there was no younger son of the Rensselaerswyck line who left issue. Until within recent times, therefore, its activities were restricted to a very few members, and its record, comparatively viewed, is not one of much range or diversity of personal interests or careers.

(187)

On the other hand, the Van Rensselaers of Greenbush and Claverack were from the beginning a prolific family. In the third generation from Hendrick, the immediate progenitor of this branch—which coincided with revolutionary times,—his male descendants had already become quite numerous. The record given on a previous page strikingly shows the numerical superiority of the junior branch at that period; all the twelve Van Rensselaers who served in the revolutionary armies being of this family, as the senior branch (though of equal patriotism and military spirit) had no member of an age to bear arms. The line of Hendrick has maintained to the present time its decided advantage in numbers; and not alone in its male descent, but in its ramifications on the female side, is of far greater scope than the elder stock. It has naturally resulted that the superiority is also with the cadet branch in the aggregate of distinguished and noteworthy individualities; and in the matter of connections by marriage—of essential genealogical consequence—the younger line presents aspects quite as interesting and important as the elder.

I

KILIAEN VAN RENSSELAER of Amsterdam, Holland, born about 1595, died 1646; first patroon of Rensselaerswyck; married, 2d, Anna Van Wely. Their second son was

II

JEREMIAS VAN RENSSELAER, born in Holland about 1632, died at Rensselaerswyck, October 12, 1674 (n. s.); third patroon of Rensselaerswyck; married, July 12, 1662, Maria Van Cortlandt, daughter of Oloff Stevense and Annetje (Loockermans) Van Cortlandt. Their youngest son (fourth child) was

III

HENDRICK VAN RENSSELAER, born at Watervliet, N. Y., October 23, 1667. In conformity with English usages concerning the succession to estates, a patent of confirmation of the entire manor of Rensselaerswyck was issued to his elder brother Kiliaen on the 20th of May, 1704. Hendrick's right of inheritance was, however, recognized by Kiliaen in a deed of conveyance, executed June 1, 1704, by which the younger brother received the so-called "Lower" or "Eastern" Manor of Claverack, situated in the present Columbia County, N. Y., together with a tract opposite Albany, called Greenbush, and an island in the Hudson River; the Claverack Manor consisting of about sixty thousand and the Greenbush tract of eighteen hundred acres. Greenbush (from the Dutch *bet Greyne Bosch*) was a densely wooded strip running two miles back into Rensselaer County, and was a portion of the original purchase of the first patroon from the Indians. Claverack (from *Klever-ack,* clover field) was acquired later in two purchases, the first being made in 1649 by Brandt Van Slichtenhorst, vice director, and the second in 1670 by Jeremias Van Rensselaer.

With the Greenbush lands Hendrick became the owner of the historic mansion of the Van Rensselaers, "Fort Crailo." This house was built in 1642, the date being established by an inscription on a stone in the foundation walls: "K. V. R. 1642 Anno Domini." An opposite stone bears the name, "Do. Megapolensis," commemorating doubtless the coming of that celebrated divine, who, with his wife and children, sailed from Amsterdam in the patroon's ship in June, 1642. "Fort Crailo" was so called for the patroon's estate of "Crailo," near Huizen, in Holland. The dwelling was occupied originally by the Van Rensselaer agents who administered the colony in the absence of any member of the family. It was a massive structure, pierced with stone portholes for defense, two of which, in the front wall, are still to be seen. According to Brodhead, when the Indians attacked and massacred many of the inhabitants of Wiltwyck, June 17, 1663, the farmers fled to the "patroons's new fort Crailo at Greenbush for protection;" and tradition says that it sustained several Indian sieges.

Hendrick Van Rensselaer established his residence in the old mansion, making various improvements. His eldest son and successor, Colonel Johannes Van Rensselaer, built, about 1740, an extensive addition, and, as thus reconstructed, "Fort Crailo" has continued, without material external alteration, to the present time. From Colonel Johannes the house passed in 1783 to his grandson, John Jeremias. After the latter's death (1829) it was occupied under lease by various persons until 1852, when his son, Dr. Jeremiah, removed to it with his family. Dr. Jeremiah's widow, inheriting the property, continued there for some years, when it was sold to strangers. Recently, through the efforts principally of Mrs. Susan de Lancey Van Rensselaer Strong (a descendant of Hendrick Van Rensselaer), it has been purchased and arrangements have been made for its permanent preservation.[8]

During the early generations of the junior branch the chief residence was "Fort Crailo;" but another mansion was built by Hendrick Van Rensselaer on the Claverack Manor, where also the family flourished and multiplied. The principal name associated with the Claverack estate is that of Brigadier-General Robert Van Rensselaer.

Although the share of the family possessions received by Hendrick was small compared with that of his elder broth-

----

[8] For the historical particulars of this ancient mansion we are indebted to a pamphlet published several years ago by Mrs. Strong, entitled "Fort Crailo, the Greenbush Manor House."

"Fort Crailo" has been described as "the first house of the Van Rensselaer Family built in America, and undoubtedly the oldest continuously inhabited dwelling in the state of New York." In colonial times and afterwards it was noted for a liberal and refined hospitality, and many of the most celebrated characters in American history have been among the guests entertained. It was here that the lines of "Yankee Doodle" were composed.

er, it was large, even for those times, measured by other and more representative standards. Besides, says Mrs. Strong, "the rich and fertile lands of Claverack were superior to the rocky soil of the Helderbergs. The sixty thousand acres of Claverack and the eighteen hundred of Greenbush brought forth abundantly under thrifty and diligent management. The many scions of the cadet branch were well portioned off with large and productive farms."

Previously to coming into his inheritance Hendrick Van Rensselaer had sought to acquire a domain of his own by the purchase from the Indians (1698) of the Schaghticoke Tract, six miles square, on the Hudson River; but owing to a claim of previous right of purchase advanced by the city of Albany, he eventually resigned this property. He was Indian commissioner for thirty years, member of the town council of Albany, and representative in the assembly.

Died at "Fort Crailo," July 4, 1740.

Married, March 19, 1689, Catharine (Annatje) Van Brugh, daughter of Johannes Van Brugh and Catharine Roeloffe Jans—the latter being a daughter of Annake Jans. Johannes Van Brugh was one of the schepens of New Amsterdam and a man of large wealth. A silver cup bequeathed by Anneke Jans to her daughter, Catharine Roeloffe Van Brugh, is still in the possession of the descendants of the latter's daughter, Mrs. Hendrick Van Rensselaer.

Issue:

1. Maria Van Rensselaer. M. Samuel Ten Broeck.
2. Catharine Van Rensselaer. M. Johannes Ten Broeck.
3. Anna Van Rensselaer. M. Peter Douw.
4. Elizabeth Van Rensselaer. M. John Richard.
5. Helena Van Rensselaer. M. Jacob Wendell.
6. Jeremias Van Rensselaer, d. young.
7. *Johannes Van Rensselaer;* of whom below.
8. Hendrick Van Rensselaer, known as Colonel Henry Van Rensselaer, b. May 8, 1712, d. July 9, 1793. In the Revolution he was "one of the two old men who could not go to the war." M., 1st, October 16, 1735, Elizabeth Van Brugh; 2d, November 20, 1762, Mrs. Alida (Livingston) Rutsen, widow of Jacob Rutsen, daughter

of Gilbert Livingston, and mother (by her first husband) of Cornelia Rutsen, who m. General Robert Van Rensselaer. Issue of Hendrick Van Rensselaer (all by his first marriage:)

i. Hendrick Van Rensselaer, d. unmarried.

ii. Johannes Van Rensselaer, d. young.

iii. Jeremias Van Rensselaer, b. July 15, 1740, d. February 19, 1810; lieutenant of the Second Regiment of the New York line in the Revolution, paymaster to the end of the war, and lieutenant-governor of New York, 1804-10. M. Helen Lansing; had one son (who did not marry) and three daughters; his eldest daughter, Elizabeth, m. (as his second wife) Peter E. Elmendorf.

iv. Margaretta Van Rensselaer. M. Francis Nicoll.

v. Johannes Van Rensselaer, b. September 23, 1742, d. June 23, 1802; a commissioned colonel in the Revolution. M. Frances Nicoll; no issue.

vi. Catharine Van Rensselaer. M. Harmanus Wendell.

vii. David Van Rensselaer, b. July 18, 1749, d. June 19, 1798; a commissioned major in the Revolution. M. Maria Schuyler; no issue.

viii. Killian Van Rensselaer, twin with the preceding; d. December 14, 1849; a commissioned lieutenant in the Revolution. M. Maria White. Two daughters, both of whom married.

ix. Peter Van Rensselaer, b. December 24, 1751, d. April 23, 1816. M., April 7, 1782, Maria Ten Broeck. Two of his children married: Elizabeth Van Rensselaer, m. Wessel Ten Broeck, and

Henry P. Van Rensselaer, b. October 8, 1794, d. January 25, 1874. He was the only male of this branch now represented by descendants. M., October 19, 1815, Jane A. Fort. Besides other children, they had four sons who left issue, as follows: Peter Van Rensselaer, m. Ann Truax; Abram Van Rensselaer, m. Sarah A. How; Vrooman Van Rensselaer, m. Mary Throop; and John Van Rensselaer, m. Eunice A. Power.

9. Kiliaen (Killian) Van Rensselaer, b. 1717, d. December 28, 1781. He was commissioned colonel of the Fourth Regiment, Albany County militia, on the 1st of April, 1778, and served to the end of the war; was a member of the Albany committee of correspondence, 1775; representative in the New York assembly for several terms, beginning in 1779. He died, writes a descendant, "leaving to his children an unblemished reputation for integrity, honor, and patriotism." M., 1st, January 7, 1742, Ariantje (Harriet) Schuyler, daughter of Nicholas Schuyler and Elsie Wendell, and has seven children: Hendrick, Philip, Nicholas, Killian K., Catharine (m. William Ludlow), Elsie (m. Abraham A. Lansing), and Maria (m. Leonard Gansevoort, Jr.). Sons:

i. Hendrick Van Rensselaer (called Henry K.), lieutenant-colonel and colonel in the Revolution; "defended Fort Ann with an unequal force with great bravery and obstinacy, in support of the retreat of our troops from Ticonderoga, July, 1777"; was badly wounded in this affair and made lame for life; d. 1816. He left a son, the noted Major-General Solomon Van Rensselaer (b. at Greenbush, August 6, 1774), who at the age of eighteen served as cornet in Wayne's expedition, was promoted to the command of a troop at the age of twenty, fought with much distinction throughout the War of 1812, and was appointed by Governor DeWitt Clinton brevet major-general of New York militia. General Solomon Van Rensselaer m. his first cousin, Harriet Van Rensselaer, daughter of Lieutenant-Colonel Philip Van Rensselaer (below); they resided at "Cherry Hill," a property below "The Flatts" (Albany) which belonged to her (Harriet's) mother. The daughter of General Solomon and Harriet Van Rensselaer, named Harriet Maria Van Rensselaer, inherited "Cherry Hill" from her grandmother; she m. Peter Edward Elmendorf and left a daughter, Harriet Van Rensselaer Elmendorf, who m. John W. Gould. This last couple live in Newark, N. J., and have issue one son, Edmund Westerlo Gould; he m. Elizabeth Tripp, their issue being Edmund Elmendorf Gould and Catharine Livingston Gould. "Cherry Hill" is now owned and occupied by Edward M. Rankin, a well-known lawyer of Albany, whose wife is a descendant of Robert S. Van Rensselaer, son of Lieutenant-Colonel Philip Van Rensselaer (who built the house); it has been carefully restored.

ii. Philip Van Rensselaer, lieutenant-colonel in the Revolution on the general staff of the ordnance department, his commission being received from General Philip Schuyler and confirmed by congress; had charge of the military stores of the northern department during the war; was also a member of the committee of safety of Albany.

iii. Nicholas Van Rensselaer, captain in Goos Van Schaick's regiment, New York line, to the end of the Revolution.

iv. Killian K. Van Rensselaer, b. at the Greenbush Manor House, June 9, 1763, d. June 18, 1845; educated at Yale; admitted to the New York bar in 1784; district attorney of Columbia County, active in military affairs, and member of congress for several terms; lived after his marriage at Albany. M., January 27, 1791, Margaretta Sanders, daughter of John Sanders of Scotia; a son was John Sanders Van Rensselaer of Albany, who had a son, the late Rev. Maunsell Van Rensselaer, D. D., author of "Annals of the Van Rensselaers of the United States, Especially as they Relate to the Family of Killian K.

Van Rensselaer" (1888). Another descendant of this line was the late Mrs. Catharine Van. Rensselaer Bonney, author of the very notable work, "A Legacy of Historical Gleanings" (1875).

Colonel Killian Van Rensselaer, youngest son of Hendrick, m., 2d, September 18, 1769, Maria Low; no issue.

IV

COLONEL JOHANNES VAN RENSSELAER, eldest son of Hendrick and Catharine (Van Brugh) Van Rensselaer, was born in the "Fort Crailo" Manor House, February 11, 1708. He inherited Greenbush and Claverack from his father, residing throughout his long life at "Fort Crailo," where all his children were born. As early as 1737 when he was a member of the twenty-first provincial assembly of New York, he ranged himself on the side of the radicals. In 1743 he was appointed captain of a company of foot, later being promoted to colonel. He was an active supporter of American independence, though too old to take a personal part in the Revolutionary War. But his youngest brother, Killian, three of his sons, and eight of his nephews held commissions in the continental army. In June, 1775, the American troops, while on the march to Ticonderoga, held their cantonment on his grounds; and in 1777 his residence was for a time the headquarters of the northern army, commanded by his son-in-law, General Philip Schuyler.

Died in the summer of 1783.

Married, 1st, January 3, 1734, Angelica Livingston.

Issue:

1. Catharine Van Rensselaer, b. 1734. M., September 17, 1755, Philip Schuyler, afterward major-general, United States senator from New York, etc.

2. *Jeremias Van Rensselaer;* of whom below.

3. *Robert Van Rensselaer;* of whom below.

4. Hendrick Johannes Van Rensselaer, b. October 23, 1742 (o. s.), d. at the Claverack Manor House, March 22, 1814. Before the Revolution he was captain in the company of foot in the British

army of which his father was colonel. In 1777 he was commissioned colonel in the continental forces. "The food supply for the northern army under General Schuyler was raised in the Claverack Manor, and it was the duty of Colonel Henry J. Van Rensselaer from 1776 to 1783 to induce the tenants to remain on the manor to plant and cultivate the land, and then dispose of their produce to him upon faith of future payments by a revolutionary government." M., November 16, 1765, Rachel Douw, daughter of his cousin, Volkert P. Douw. Seven children. His eldest son, Johannes Hendrick Van Rensselaer (known as John H.), was b. March 8, 1768, m., 1798, Elizabeth, daughter of Harmanus Wendell of Albany, and had an only son, Hendrick Johannes Van Rensselaer (known as young Henry J.), who was b. January 21, 1806, m., May 5, 1830, Susan, daughter of Robert A. Barnard of Hudson, N. Y., and d. September 10, 1874. A descendant, Hendrick, Johannes Van Rensselaer Barnard, is now living in the Claverack Manor House, built (1704-8) by the first Hendrick Van Rensselaer. Another descendant in the line of Colonel Hendrick Johannes Van Rensselaer, Miss Elizabeth Wendell Van Rensselaer, resides in Hudson, N. Y., and possesses many rare and interesting family relics.

5. *James Van Rensselaer;* of whom below.

Colonel Johannes Van Rensselaer married, 2d, Gertrude Van Cortlandt.

V

JEREMIAS VAN RENSSELAER, eldest son of Johannes and Angelica (Livingston) Van Rensselaer, was born at "Fort Crailo" in 1738. Owing to his early death, many years before that of his father, he did not succeed to the family estates, his position as the principal heir, however, being succeeded to by his only son.

Died in 1769.

Married, July 3, 1758, Judith Bayard.

Issue:

1. *John Jeremias Van Rensselaer;* of whom below.

GENERAL ROBERT VAN RENSSELAER, second son of Johannes and Angelica (Livingston) Van Rensselaer, was born at "Fort Crailo," December 16, 1740, being named for his maternal grandfather, Robert Livingston, Jr. He resided in the Manor House at Claverack.

In common with all of his family who were able to bear arms during the Revolution, Robert was in the military service of his country, and his is the most distinguished Van Rensselaer name identified with that war. The commission of colonel of the Eighth Regiment, Albany County militia, was issued to him on the 20th of October, 1775, and that of brigadier-general, Second Brigade, Albany County militia, on June 16, 1780. He fought at Ticonderoga under the orders of his brother-in-law, General Philip Schuyler, and commanded the militia which pursued and defeated Sir John Johnston when on his famous raid in the Mohawk Valley in 1780.

From 1775 to 1777 he was the representative in the New York provincial congress of the Eastern Manor (comprising Greenbush and Claverack).

Died at the Claverack Manor House, September 11, 1802, and was buried with distinguished honors from the city of Hudson close beside the wall of the Claverack Church. The *Balance and Columbian Repository,* of Hudson, in an account of his large military funeral, said: "General Van Rensselaer was a zealous and active officer during the Revolutionary War, and since the peace has discharged the duties of a military and civil officer with honor to himself and advantage to the community. In private life his virtues secured to him esteem as his public services commanded general approbation. His residence at Claverack Manor was a place of refuge for many afflicted settlers on the Mohawk when flying from the incursions of the Indian allies of the British. To the poor and needy his heart and purse were never closed."

Married, April 23, 1765, Cornelia Rutsen, daughter of Colonel Jacob and Alida (Livingston) Rutsen; she was born 1747 and died January 31, 1790.

Issue:

1. John Van Rensselaer, b. 1766, d. in early manhood. M. Angelica Van Rensselaer, daughter of Colonel Henry and Rachel (Douw) Van Rensselaer of Claverack; no issue. His widow m., 2d, John C. Schuyler, and 3d, Derrick Lane, by whom she had a son and daughter.

2. *Jacob Rutsen Van Rensselaer;* of whom below.

3. *Jeremias Van Rensselaer;* of whom below.

4. Alida Van Rensselaer, d. March, 1799. M., in 1793, Elisha Kane, son of John and Sybil (Kent) Kane.

5. Catharine Van Rensselaer, b. about 1770-1, d. February 2, 1867. M. Colonel John Arent Schuyler of Belleville, N. J. Issue:

i. Angelica Van Rensselaer Schuyler, b. 1810, d. March, 1864; "a woman of fine abilities and great strength of character."

ii. John Arent Schuyler, b. 1811, d. November 21, 1855. M. Frances Elizabeth Bleecker, daughter of Alexander Bleecker of Brooklyn, N. Y.; no issue.

iii. Robert Van Rensselaer Schuyler, b. 1813, d. February 19, 1855. M. Kate Mancini of New York. Issue:

1. Van Rensselaer Schuyler, b. July 27, 1852; resides in New York City. M., June 26, 1899, Ethel Cornelia Paul, daughter of Cornelius Danforth Paul of New York City.

iv. Catharine Gertrude Schuyler, b. January 15, 1815, d. October 8, 1881. M., October 4, 1838, Henry S. Craig.

v. Jacob Rutsen Schuyler, b. February 23, 1816, d. February 4, 1887; head of the firm of Schuyler, Hartley and Graham, manufacturers of arms for the United States government during the Civil War, with works at Bridgeport, Conn.; resided at Bergen Point, N. J. (now Bayonne). M., November 18, 1847, Susanna Haigh Edwards. Issue:

1. Sarah Edwards Schuyler, b. April 6, 1849, d. May 30, 1897.

2. Katharine Van Rensselaer Schuyler, b. August 13, 1855, d. December 10, 1892. M., March 20, 1879, Henry Thornton Imbrie of Jersey City. Issue: Henry Thornton Imbrie and Schuyler Imbrie.

3. Rutsen Van Rensselaer Schuyler, b. February 4, 1853. M., 1st, February 4, 1872, Augusta H. Mellick; 2d, April 3, 1889, Mary Amelia Hall. Issue (by first marriage): Rutsen Van Rensselaer Schuyler, Jr., and Sarah Edwards Schuyler; (by second marriage): Marguerite Van Rensselaer Schuyler and Janet Smiley Schuyler.

4. Edwards Ogden Schuyler, b. May 23, 1863, d. January 4, 1905. M., October 12, 1887, Georgia A. de Fontaine. Issue: Katharine Van Rensselaer Schuyler and Sarah Edwards Schuyler.

5. Susanna Edwards Schuyler, b. March 10, 1863, d. January 10, 1903. M., February 8, 1887, Nicholas Murray Butler, now president of Columbia University. Issue: Sarah Schuyler Butler.

6. Angelica Van Rensselaer Schuyler, b. January 23, 1870. M., October 5, 1892, De Lagnal Haigh; they reside at Summit, N. J. Issue: Angelica Van Rensselaer Haigh, Rebecca Mac Rae Haigh, and Thomas Devereux Haigh.

6. Angelica Van Rensselaer, b. about 1785, d. at "Mount Schuyler," Belleville, N. J., the residence of her sister, Mrs. John Arent Schuyler, November 23, 1818. M., February 11, 1813, Rev. Thomas Yardley How. Issue:

i. Robert Field How, b. November 15, 1813, d. at Brownville, N. Y., August, 1835.

ii. Jacob Rutsen Van Rensselaer How, b. December 6, 1814, d. at Auburn, N. Y., May 12, 1865. Issue:

1. Catharine Van Rensselaer How, d. May, 1903.

2. Clara A. How, resides in Buffalo, N. Y.

3. Fanny How.

iii. Angelica Van Rensselaer How, b. April 23, 1817, d. in Auburn, N. Y., February, 1901. M. Judge Hulbert of Auburn, N. Y.; no issue.

7. *Henry Van Rensselaer;* of whom below.

8. *James Van Rensselaer;* of whom below.

MAJOR JAMES VAN RENSSELAER, youngest son of Colonel Johannes and Angelica (Livingston) Van Rensselaer, was born at "Fort Crailo" in 1747. He was aide-de-camp, with the rank of captain, to Major-General Richard Montgomery from August to December, 1775, serving through the Canadian campaign at Fort Chambly, St. John's, Montreal, and Quebec. In April, 1776, he became captain in the Second Regiment of the New York line under Colonel James Clinton, and from June to August of the same year was aide-de-camp, with the rank of major, to General Philip Schuyler, in the northern army.

Died at "Crystal Hall," February 1, 1827.

Married, 1st, Catharine Van Cortlandt.

Issue:

1. John Van Rensselaer, b. at "Crystal Hall," 1784; was possessed of large means, and was one of the most prominent members of the Van Rensselaer Family of his times; removed to Belleville, N. J., where the related family of the Arent Schuyler line re-

sided, and where he d. in 1870. M. Elizabeth Van Cortlandt (who was b. 1787, d. 1868). Issue:

    i. James Van Rensselaer, b. 1812, d. 1840. M. Margaret Duxbury (who was b. 1810, d. 1879). Issue:

        1. James Van Rensselaer. M. Margaret Rutgers Birch. Issue: i. Elizabeth Van Cortlandt Van Rensselaer, b. 1868; m. Charles Boel of Antwerp, Belgium. ii. Sarah Schuyler Van Rensselaer, b. 1870. iii. James Henry Van Rensselaer, b. 1872; m. Florence N. Smillie (their children being Florence Van Rensselaer, b. 1900, and Bayard Van Cortlandt Van Rensselaer, b. 1903). iv. Marie Antoinette Van Rensselaer, b. 1874; m. Fritz Unger (their children being Margaret Van Rensselaer Unger, b. 1900, and Schuyler Van Rensselaer Unger, b. 1902). v. Margaret Rutgers Van Rensselaer, b. 1878; m. Dr. Antonie Voislawsky (who was b. in Poland). vi. Rebecca Coffin Van Rensselaer, b. 1885.

        ii. Stephen Van Cortlandt Van Rensselaer. M. Sarah Schuyler. Issue, Stephen Van Cortlandt Van Rensselaer, d. young.

        iii. Catharine Van Cortlandt Van Rensselaer. M. her cousin, Gratz Van Rensselaer (see below).

Major James Van Rensselaer married, 2ud, June 24, 1789, Mrs. Elsie (Schuyler) Bogert (who was born February 5, 1760, and died September 26, 1838). She was the widow of Dr. Nicholas Bogert of New York, daughter of Nicholas and Elsie (Wendell) Schuyler, and sister of Ariantje Schuyler, who married Colonel Killian Van Rensselaer, son of Hendrick.

Issue:

    2. Angelica Van Rensselaer.

    3. Philip Schuyler Van Rensselaer, b. 1797. M. Henrietta Ann Schuyler, daughter of John H. Schuyler and granddaughter of Harmanus. One son,

        Gratz Van Rensselaer, b. 1834. M. Catharine Van Cortlandt Van Rensselaer, daughter of James, son of John and Elizabeth (Van Cortlandt) Van Rensselaer. Issue:

        1. Philip Schuyler Van Rensselaer, d. unmarried.

        2. Cortlandt Schuyler Van Rensselaer, b. in New York City; graduated from Hobart College and the Columbia Law School; lawyer in Eau Claire, Wis., and subsequently in New York, serving as assistant United States district attorney in the latter city; now identified with financial interests in New York, where he resides; member of prom-

inent clubs and patriotic organizations. M., 1891, Horace Macaulay, daughter of William Macaulay. Issue: i. Cortlandt Van Rensselaer, b. 1900.

    3. Elizabeth Van Rensselaer. M. Dr. George L. Hull. Issue, George L. Hull, Jr.

    4. John Van Rensselaer, M. D., resides in Washington, D. C. M. Mary Johnston.

    5. Margaret Van Rensselaer.

4. James Van Rensselaer, d. unmarried.

VI

Line of Jeremias Van Rensselaer (V.)

JOHN JEREMIAS VAN RENSSELAER, only son of Jeremias and Judith (Bayard) Van Rensselaer, was born at "Fort Crailo," about 1769. Under the will of his grandfather, Colonel Johannes Van Rensselaer, he inherited the Greenbush lands, with the ancient mansion, which he remodelled in its interior. He served as lieutenant-colonel of the Fourteenth Regiment, Albany County militia.

Died September 22, 1828.

Married Catharine Glen.

Issue:

    1. Catharine Glen Van Rensselaer, d. 1866. M. Nanning Visscher, son of Colonel Visscher of the British army; no issue.

    2. John Jeremias Van Rensselaer, d. young.

    3. Dr. Jeremias Van Rensselaer, b. 1796, d. 1871; resided during his last years at "Fort Crailo." M., 1st, Charlotte Foster; 2d, Annie F. Waddington. Issue (by first marriage):

        i. Jeremias Van Rensselaer, b. 1824, d. 1866. M. Julia Jaudon. Issue:

            1. Augustus Van Cortlandt Van Rensselaer, present head of the Greenbush and Claverack branch of the Van Rensselaer Family; resides at "Fair Acres," Stockbridge, Mass.

            2. Peyton J. Van Rensselaer, resides at 16 East Thirty-second Street, New York.

        ii. Francis Van Rensselaer, b. 1829, d. 1871. M., 1851, Anne G. Moore. Issue:

            1. Foster Van Rensselaer, d. 1871.

            2. Glen Van Rensselaer, b. 1867, d. 1886.

    4. Glen Van Rensselaer, b. 1798, d. 1871.

5. Cornelius Van Rensselaer, b. 1801; d. June, 1871. M., October 31, 1826, Catharine Westerlo Bleecker, daughter of John Bleecker and Elizabeth Van Rensselaer (who was the daughter of Stephen Van Rensselaer IV.). Issue:

i. John Van Rensselaer, d. young.

ii. Stephen Bleecker Van Rensselaer, d. young.

iii. Cornelia Van Rensselaer, b. 1831. M., 1856, Rev. Cornelius Winter Bolton of Pelham, N. Y.

iv. Katharine Westerlo Van Rensselaer, b. 1834.

v. Dr. John Van Rensselaer, b. 1836; resides at Swartswood, N. J. M., 1864, Florence Taylor. Issue:

1. Lyndsay Van Rensselaer, b. 1870. M. Lolita A. Coffin. Issue, Catharine Glen Van Rensselaer.

2. Florence Van Rensselaer.

6. Visscher Van Rensselaer; resides in Rensselaer, N. Y. M., September 3, 1866, Mary Augusta Miller. Issue:

i. Katharine Westerlo Van Rensselaer, b. September 3, 1867, d. February 12, 1896. M., January 23, 1894, Benjamin Walworth Arnold of Albany, N. Y. Issue, Katharine Van Rensselaer Arnold, b. January 28, 1896.

ii. Cornelius Glen Van Rensselaer, b. September 24, 1869. M., 1898, Genevieve Vessell. Issue:

1. Katharine Stewart Van Rensselaer, b. 1903.

iii. Cornelia Livingston Van Rensselaer, b. June 5, 1879. M., March 21, 1900, Hon. Theodore Strong of New Brunswick, N. J., son of Hon. Woodbridge and Harriet A. (Hartwell) Strong and brother of Alan Hartwell Strong (below). Mr. Strong is a lawyer at New Brunswick, is active in politics, was formerly state senator of New Jersey, and is at present a member of the state board of railroad assessors. Issue:

1. Theodore Strong, b. January 3, 1901.

2. Cornelia Livingston Van Rensselaer Strong, b. November 16, 1902.

3. Katharine Van Rensselaer Strong, b. November 10, 1904.

Line of General Robert Van Rensselaer (V.)

COLONEL JACOB RUTSEN VAN RENSSELAER, second son of General Robert and Cornelia (Rutsen) Van Rensselaer, was born in 1767. He resided at Hudson, N. Y.

He possessed large means, and exercised an important influence in the affairs of New York State, was a member of the legislature (his term expiring in June, 1812,) was actively interested in the building of the Erie Canal, and was associated with Governor De Witt Clinton and Abraham Varick in this undertaking and business ventures. According to an old letter, dated June 17, 1812, he was at that time expecting orders to march to Niagara, and was "spoken of among a number of his party friends as a candidate for the office of governor of this state the ensuing election."

Married Cornelia de Peyster, daughter of Pierre de Peyster.

Issue:

1. Cornelia Van Rensselaer, d. young.
2. Pierre Van Rensselaer, d. young.
3. Cornelia Van Rensselaer, d. at the age of nineteen.
4. Pierre Van Rensselaer, d. at about the age of twenty-five.
5. Jacob Rutsen Van Rensselaer. M., 1848, Emily Denning of Fishkill, N. Y. Issue.
    i. Emily Denning Van Rensselaer.
6. Robert Schuyler Van Rensselaer, b. about 1810' d. about 1874; resided at Bordentown, N. J.; president of the Camden and Amboy Railroad. M. Virginia Kidd. Issue:
    i. Virginia Van Rensselaer. M. Robert Kidd. They reside at New Brighton, Staten Island.
    ii. Robert Schuyler Van Rensselaer, b. 1851; graduated at Yale; civil engineer. M. Arrietta Archer. Issue:
        1. Le Roy Van Rensselaer.
7. Jeremiah Van Rensselaer, b. 1812, d. July 8, 1874, in New Brunswick, N. J. He was interested in railways, and was the founder of Dodd's Express. M. Mary Fleming, daughter of Gilbert Fleming. Issue:
    i. James Fleming Van Rensselaer, b. December 4, 1844, d. January 3, 1900. M., February 7, 1866, Annie J. Harriman, sister of E. H. Harriman. His widow resides in Los Angeles, Cal. Issue:
        1. Jeremiah Van Rensselaer, b. October 27, 1866. M., November, 1889, Virginia Robinson. Issue: i. Franklyn Robinson Van Rensselaer, b. August 18, 1890. ii. Jeremiah Van Rensselaer, b. July 27, 1893. iii. William Beverley Van Rensselaer, b. October 22, 1896.
        2. Cornelia Neilson Van Rensselaer, b. April 4, 1868.
        3. Orlando Harriman Van Rensselaer, b. March 13, 1870. M. Minnie Louise Kramer. Issue: i. Robert Schuyler Van Rensselaer, b. September 19, 1900. ii. Evelyn Lucile Van Rensselaer, b. April 23, 1902.
        4. Rutsen Schuyler Van Rensselaer, b. March 16, 1872, d. December 31, 1875.

5. Mary Fleming Van Rensselaer, b. April 18, 1874, d. June 21, 1875.

6. James Fleming Van Rensselaer, b. August 18, 1875. M., October 8, 1903, Jane Boylan Glover of Augusta, Ga. Issue: i. Katrina Van Rensselaer, b. June 8, 1905.

7. Anna Harriman Van Rensselaer, b. August 31, 1877. M., October 8, 1904, Louis Cuthbert Masten of Omaha, Neb. Issue: i. Anna Harriman Masten, b. December 20, 1905.

8. Katrina Van Rensselaer, b. May 29, 1879. M., July 17, 1902, Maurice Edwin Ginn of Boston. Issue: i. Katrina Van Rensselaer Ginn, b. September 16, 1903; d. January 23, 1905.

9. Mary Frances Van Rensselaer, b. May 1, 1881. M., February 21, 1906, Rufus Janvier Briscoe, Jr.

10. Robert Schuyler Van Rensselaer, b. May 27, 1882, d. December 13, 1890.

8. Catharine Van Rensselaer. She was a very beautiful and accomplished young woman, who died of grief for the loss of her father; and the affliction of Catharine's death was the direct cause of the decease of her eldest sister, Cornelia. The story of these sisters has been long told in the family, and is preserved in the "Recollections" of the late Miss Cornelia Rutsen Van Rensselaer of New Brunswick, N. J.

JEREMIAS VAN RENSSELLAER, third son of General Robert and Cornelia (Rutsen) Van Rensselaer, was born at the Greenbush Manor House in 1769. He resided many years at Utica, N. Y., where he was one of the most prominent citizens and actively identified with commercial enterprise, being the head of the firm of Van Rensselaer and Kane, which transacted a great business in bringing grain from the west and also had a large trade in coffee and spices from the West Indies. A branch of the house was located at St. Croix, under the charge of the Cidwises (relatives of Jeremias Van Rensselaer's wife) and of John Cullen (brother of the wife of James Van Rensselaer, Jr.). In one of the financial panics which prostrated the trade of the country Mr. Van Rensselaer's firm failed. He then removed to Canandaigua, N. Y., where he died in January, 1827.

Married, about 1797, Sybil Adeline Kane of Albany,

daughter of John and Sybil (Kent) Kane. The family connections and associations involved in this marriage are of much interest. As seen under V., Alida Van Rensselaer, a sister of Jeremias, also married a Kane (Elisha, brother of Jeremias's wife). John Kane, the American progenitor of the Kane Family, came about the middle of the eighteenth century from County Antrim, Ireland, where are still to be seen the ruins of Dunseverick Castle, the ancient family seat of the O'Kanes or O'Cahans. Accompanying John Kane to this country was Charles Cullen of County Ulster; and the two friends married daughters of Rev. Elisha Kent. Charles Cullen and his wife died in their early prime, and their daughter ''Patty'' (named for Martha de Lancey) also died at an early age. Thereupon the other Cullen children, Susan de Lancey Cullen and John Kane Cullen, were taken by their aunt, Mrs. Kane of Albany, whose daughter, Sybil Adeline Kane, married Jeremias Van Rensselaer of Utica. Mrs. Kane, when her death was approaching, desired that her young niece, Susan de Lancey Cullen, should live with her daughter, Mrs. Jeremias Van Rensselaer of Utica; and from this arrangement resulted eventually the marriage of Miss Cullen with James Van Rensselaer, the youngest brother of Jeremias; Miss Cullen's brother, John Kane Cullen, being provided for meanwhile by the West Indian agency of the house of Van Rensselaer and Kane. As seen below, the eldest daughter of Jeremias and Sybil Adeline (Kane) Van Rensselaer, married Francis Granger, postmaster-general of the United States, and it was to be with this daughter that Jeremias Van Rensselaer removed to Canandaigua (the home of the Grangers). The most close and tender intimacy was maintained by Jeremias with the family of his brother, James, in Utica (the wives being first cousins). James's daughter, Cornelia Rutsen Van Rensselaer, who died recently at New Brunswick, N. J., in her ninety-third year, was educated in the family of Jere-

mias at Canandaigua, and has told and written most
graphic accounts of the life there.

Issue:

1. Cornelia Rutsen Van Rensselaer, b. about 1798 in Utica, N.
Y., d. before her parents. She was a singularly beautiful and accomplished lady. M. Francis Granger, subsequently postmaster-
general. Issue:

i. Gideon Granger, d. November, 1905. M. Antoinette
Isaphene Pierson of Ramapo, N. Y., (who d. November, 1903).
Issue: Antoinette Granger and Isaphene Granger (both resid-
ing in Canandaigua).

ii. Adele Granger. M. John Thayer of Boston, Mass.
(brother of Nathaniel Thayer, who m. Cornelia Van Rensselaer, daughter of Stephen Van Rensselaer IV. of the Rensselaerswyck line). Issue: Adele Granger Thayer, who now resides in Boston.—Mrs. Adele (Granger) Thayer m., 2d, Hon.
Robert C. Winthrop.

2. Alida Van Rensselaer, b. in Utica, 1800, d. at "The Hermitage," Mount Morris, Livingston County, N. Y., March 8, 1832.
M., May 9, 1820, Judge Charles Holker Carroll (who was b. May
4, 1794, d. July 22, 1865, a descendant of the Carrolls of Carroll-
ton). Issue: six children, of whom only two survived to maturity
and had descendants, as follows:

i. Cornelia Granger Carroll, b. at "The Hermitage,"
August 4, 1826. M., May 15, 1850, Edward P. Fuller; they reside in Grand Rapids, Mich. Issue:

1. Sophia Fuller, b. October 14, 1857. M., April 26,
1876, Edwin F. Sweet, now mayor of Grand Rapids; their
children being: i. Carroll Fuller Sweet, b. June 24, 1877;
graduated at Yale, 1899. ii. George Fuller Sweet, b. November 4, 1881; graduated at the University of Michigan,
1904. iii. Sidney Edward Sweet, b. August 31, 1883; graduated at Yale, 1905. iv. Cornelia Van Rensselaer Sweet,
b. November 5, 1886; graduated at Dana Hall, Wellesley
College, 1904. v. Sophia Fuller Sweet, b. October 5, 1902.

2. Philo Carroll Fuller, b. March 19, 1857; graduated
at Yale, 1881; resides in Grand Rapids. M., December 25,
1882, Harriet Isabel Gilbert (who d. November 13, 1890).
Issue: i. Catharine Gilbert Fuller, b. October 12, 1884. ii.
Margaret Carroll Fuller, b. March 7, 1886. iii. Edward
Philo Fuller, b. July 1, 1887.

3. Carroll Fuller, b. October 29, 1859, d. April 9, 1872.

ii. Anne E. Carroll, b. at "The Hermitage," May 11, 1828,
d. at the residence of her sister, Mrs. Fuller, in Grand Rapids.
M., December 24, 1849, William D. Fitzhugh of "Hampton,"
Livingston County, N. Y. Issue:

1. Anne Fitzhugh, b. 1850. M., 1861, Hamilton Carroll Wright; resides in Bay City, Mich. Issue: Virginia Wright, m. Dr. Thomas L. Kane of Kane, Pa. (their children being Elizabeth Dennistoun Kane, Archibald Van Rensselaer Kane, and Sibyl Kent Kane); Hamilton Mercer Wright, m. Elizabeth Pease (their children being Hamilton Mercer Wright and Eugene Wright); Sibyl Katherine Wright, m. Dr. George S. McLandress (child, Virginia McLandress); Cornelia Fitzhugh Wright, Archibald Van Rensselaer Wright, Charles Carroll Wright, Alida Fitzhugh Wright, and William Edward Wright.

2. Alida Catharine Fitzhugh, d. in Texas.

3. Carroll Fitzhugh, d. 1880.

4. Cornelia Fitzhugh. M. Richard Conover of Princeton, N. J.; they reside in Bay City, Mich. Issue: Carroll Fitzhugh Conover, b. February 8, 1890; Helen Field Conover, b. March 21, 1898; and Alida Van Rensselaer Conover, b. February 6, 1900.

5. Edward F. D. Fitzhugh; graduated at Harvard; chemist.

3. Catharine Schuyler Van Rensselaer, b. 1802, d. about 1873. Unmarried; lived at "The Hermitage," being a second mother to her Carroll nieces.

4. Robert Van Rensselaer, b. about 1805, d. about 1840. M. Margaret Stuyvesant; no issue.

5. Archbald Kane Van Rensselaer, b. about 1808. Unmarried.

6. Jacob Rutsen Van Rensselaer, b. about 1811, d. about 1840. M. Virginia Hutchins of Norfolk, Va.; one son, Archibald Kane Van Rensselaer.—Mrs. Virginia (Hutchins) Van Rensselaer m., 2d, Hamilton Wright of New Orleans; of her children were Hamilton Mercer Wright (who m. Anne Fitzhugh above) and Nina Wright, la Marquise de Podestad.

7. James Carnahan Van Rensselaer. Unmarried.

8. Jeremiah Van Rensselaer. M. Mary Hartwell of Detroit, Mich.; no issue known.

HENRY VAN RENSSELAER, fourth son of General Robert and Cornelia (Rutsen) Van Rensselaer, was born November 8, 1775. He resided near Hudson, N. Y., his family removing after his death to Poughkeepsie.

Died November 19, 1852.

Married, November 30, 1800, Catharine D. Hoffman, sister of Samuel Verplanck Hoffman and aunt of the late Very Rev. Eugene A. Hoffman, D. D.; she was born January 14, 1779, died December 31, 1863.

Issue:
 1. Cornelia Rutsen Van Rensselaer, d. November 21, 1861. M. Robert B. Rutgers. Issue: Margaret Bayard Rutgers m. Mr. Finlay, and had children.
 2. Catharine Hoffman Van Rensselaer, b. 1803, d. May 4, 1889.
 3. Alida Van Rensselaer, b. 1805, d. February 13, 1864.
 4. Angelica Van Rensselaer, b. 1807, d. May 23, 1881. M. Rufus Reed.
 5. Charlotte M. Van Rensselaer, b. 1811, d. December 6, 1855.
 6. Adeline Van Rensselaer, b. about 1813, d. 1887.
 7. Harriet Van Rensselaer, b. about 1816, d. January 3, 1879.
 8. Herman Robert Van Rensselaer, b. about 1817, d. August 28, 1855.

JAMES VAN RENSSELAER, fifth and youngest son of General Robert and Cornelia (Rutsen) Van Rensselaer, was born at the Claverack Manor House, December 1, 1783. He lived for many years at Utica, N. Y., being a member of the house of Van Rensselaer and Kane. After the failure of that concern he removed (1835) to Indiana, for the purpose of purchasing and settling government land. He bought a large tract in what is now Jasper County, Ind., and on June 11, 1836, the title to the Falls of the Iroquois was in his name. A town was laid out soon afterward, which by act of the legislature, February 18, 1840, was named Rensselaer. It is now a city and the county seat, located on the Monon Railroad seventy miles south of Chicago. A number of the names of streets—as Susan, Cullen, Cornelia, Rutsen, and Angelica—are of family origin.

In 1840 Mr. Van Rensselaer brought his family to his new home, and they resided there until after his death (March 12, 1847). He is buried in the enclosure of the Presbyterian Church, which owes its origin to his efforts and which stands on land given by his son. The Daughters of the American Revolution have established at Rensselaer a General Van Rensselaer Chapter, in honor of James's father, General Robert.

Married, in Utica, N. Y., May 11, 1811, Susan de Lancey Cullen, daughter of Charles Cullen, Esq. (from County Ulster, Ireland), and his wife, Lucy Kent (second daughter of Rev. Elisha Kent of Mt. Carmel, Putnam County, N. Y.). Susan de Lancey (Cullen) Van Rensselaer was born October 14, 1786, at Mt. Carmel, and died June 23, 1863, at New Brunswick, N. J.

Issue:

1. *John Cullen Van Rensselaer;* of whom below.

2. Cornelia Rutsen Van Rensselaer, b. at Utica, N. Y., July 24, 1813, d. at the residence of her niece, Mrs. Alan H. Strong, at New Brunswick, N. J., January 10, 1906. The following is from a published tribute: "Miss Van Rensselaer was a woman of rare qualities of mind and heart. Her noble and unselfish character, displayed throughout her long and useful life, endeared her to a large circle of friends who will cherish her memory as that of a faithful and exemplary Christian. Born in Utica in the palmy days of that old city, in her passes a link with the early history of manorial life along the Hudson. She vividly remembered the life at Claverack Manor as early as 1826, and her unerring memory and great storytelling talent have preserved many facts of interest and value relating to life along the upper Hudson and the social intercourse among the closely allied families of the great manors during the early part of the nineteenth century."

3. Susan de Lancey Cullen Van Rensselaer, b. at Utica, December 7, 1816, d. at New Brunswick, N. J., September 22, 1870. M., August 20, 1839, at Utica, Henry Weston (b. February 12, 1806, at Sandy Hill, N. Y., d. July 1, 1880, at New Brunswick, N. J.). Issue:

    i. Van Rensselaer Weston, b. March 23, 1842, d. May 7, 1842, at Rensselaer, Ind.

    ii. Willoughby Weston, b. at Rensselaer, Ind., August 23, 1843, d. in New York City, April 26, 1902. M., 1st, in New Brunswick, N. J., October 26, 1875, Katharine Van Nest Janeway (b. March 21, 1852, d. October 11, 1900). Issue: Henry Janeway Weston, b. July 30, 1876, d. June 7, 1898.—Willoughby Weston m., 2d, Charlotte Nicoll Minton.

    iii. Rensselaer Weston, b. May 23, 1846, at Rensselaer, Ind.; graduated at Rutgers College, 1868; resides in New York City.

    iv. James Cronkhite Weston, b. at Metuchen, N. J., December 8, 1849; graduated at Rutgers College 1870; civil engineer. M., September 2, 1884, at Cornwall, N. Y., Harriet Matthiesen. Issue: Theodora Weston, b. August 26, 1885, at Galena, Alturas County, Idaho.

    v. Henry de Eresby Weston, b. at Metuchen, N. J., April

17, 1852; graduated at Rutgers, 1873, lawyer; resides in New York City.

4. Angelica (called Engeltie) Schuyler Van Rensselaer, b. at Utica, 1817, d. at Philadelphia, July 12, 1874. "One to whom long years of suffering, from childhood borne with heroic patience, taught the way of the Holy Cross, kindling in her such a flame of ardent devotion that the memorials left by the brilliant mind which dominated the frail body read like the saints of old."

VII

Line of General Robert Van Rensselaer (V.)

JOHN CULLEN VAN RENSSELAER, eldest son of James and Susan de Lancey (Cullen) Van Rensselaer, was born in Utica, N. Y., February 16, 1812. He studied law under the distinguished Judge Denio, and was admitted to the bar. In 1835 he went to Indiana with his father, the two being among the earliest pioneers of the regions along the Iroquois. He remained there until his marriage in 1838, when he returned to the east, but always continued actively interested in the town which his father founded, visiting it nearly every year.

During the greater part of his married life Mr. Van Rensselaer resided in New York City. He was known among a wide circle of friends for remarkable natural gifts and varied culture, was a brilliant raconteur, and possessed of great personal and social charm. It has been said that had he continued in the practice of his profession he might easily have won a leading place among New York lawyers.

Died at Ortley Beach, Ocean County, N. J., July 4, 1889.

Married, May 17, 1838, in Ascension Church, New York City, Cornelia Josepha Codwise.

Issue:

1. Mary Van Rensselaer, b. at No. 7 Waverly Place, New York, May 17, 1839, d. at New Brunswick, N. J., February 5, 1871. M., at Cazenovia, N. Y., September 3, 1869, Hon. Andrew Kirkpatrick Cogswell of New Brunswick, N. J., judge of the court of common pleas, grandson of Chief-Justice Andrew Kirkpatrick and also of Colonel John Bayard. Issue:

i. Andrew Kirkpatrick Cogswell, b. and d. June 21, 1868

ii. Cullen Van Rensselaer Cogswell, b. in New Brunswick, September 5, 1869; educated at St. Paul's School, Concord, N. H.; resides in New York City. M., January 1, 1896, at "Riverdale," Dedham, Mass., Agnes Eugenie Nickerson, eldest daughter of Colonel Albert Nickerson. Issue: Louisa Winslow Cogswell, b. at "Riverdale," Dedham, Mass., August 20, 1896; Mary Van Rensselaer Cogswell, b. at Southampton, Long Island, June 16, 1903.

2. Cornelia Georgina (Nina) Van Rensselaer, b. at 7 Waverly Place, New York, November 3, 1840. M., March 27, 1862, in Newport, R. I., David Olyphant Vail of Shanghai, China (b. 1834, d. April 7, 1865); resides in New York City. Issue:

i. Anna Murray Vail, b. at 60 East Thirty-sixth Street, New York, January 7, 1863; librarian of the botanical department of Columbia University, Bronx Botanic Gardens; author of several monographs on botanical subjects.

ii. Cornelia Van Rensselaer Vail, b. at 60 East Thirty-sixth Street, New York, January 23, 1865. M., February 23, 1896, Henry Golden Dearth of Providence, R. I., and Montreuil-sur-mer, Pas de Calais, France; associate-member of the National Academy of Design and member of the Society of American Artists. Issue: Cornelia Van Rensselaer Dearth, b. in Paris, France, June 11, 1896.

3. Cullen Van Rensselaer, b. at 7 Waverly Place, New York, February 28, 1843, d. April 12, 1844.

4. *Schuyler Van Rensselaer;* of whom below.

5. James Van Rensselaer, b. at 42 Clinton Place, New York, December 6, 1847, d. June 18, 1848.

6. Susan de Lancey Cullen Van Rensselaer, b. at Jamaica, Long Island, June 24, 1851; educated at Mrs. Porter's, Farmington, Conn., and in Germany and France. M., April 17, 1893, Alan Hartwell Strong of New Brunswick, N. J., son of Hon. Woodbridge Strong (now judge of the Middlesex, N. J., county court) and Harriet A. (Hartwell) Strong, and a descendant of Elder John Strong, who settled in Dorchester, Mass., in 1630. Alan Hartwell Strong was graduated from Rutgers College in 1874, admitted to the bar, and is one of the representative and able men of his profession in the state of New Jersey, having served as president of the state bar association. Mr. and Mrs. Strong reside in New Brunswick. Mrs. Strong has devoted much study to genealogical and historical subjects, and in these departments is the author of several published contributions, marked by ability and extensive information. To her the editor of this work is indebted for valuable assistance and suggestions, especially in relation to the Van Rensselaer and connecting families. No issue. Daughter by adop-

tion, Sylvia de Lancey Van Rensselaer Strong, b. at New Brunswick, N. J., October 11, 1904.

VIII

Line of General Robert Van Rensselaer (V.)

SCHUYLER VAN RENSSELAER, the only son of John Cullen and Cornelia Josepha (Codwise) Van Rennselaer who survived to maturity, was born at 42 Clinton Place, New York City, July 6, 1845. He received his early education under the tuition of Rev. C. W. Everest of Hamden, Conn., and Professor Elie Charlier of New York City, and was prepared for college by Rev. T. Thayer of Newport, R. I. In the summer of 1862 he enlisted as a private in the Newport Company of the Rhode Island Regiment, was promoted to sergeant, and was offered a commission on the staff of General Burnside. At the expiration of the four months for which he had volunteered he entered Harvard University, and was there graduated in 1867. Continuing his studies in the department of mining engineering, he was graduated from the Columbia School of Mines in 1868 and from the Mining Academy of Freiburg, Saxony, Germany, in 1871. ·

· Returning to the United States, Mr. Van Rensselaer engaged actively in his profession. He was appointed in 1877 to the position of chief engineering inspector of steel rails for the Chicago, Burlington and Quincy Railroad, continuing as such for five years, and then resigned to take up his professional practice, which he pursued from that time until his death.

In his personality Mr. Van Rensselaer was one of the worthiest representatives of his family—a man of the truest nobility of character, and equally esteemed and admired for elevation of mind and generosity of heart. In a memorial of him, published by his college class, he is thus characterized:

"His life has been a strenuous and domestic one, devoted wholly to work and to his family; and his death was well in keeping with it. Although he had many friends, only the members of the household can have appreciated him for all he was. His greatest force and charm lay in the serenity and unselfishness of his private character; and his greatest talent was the gift of common sense—the power to judge quickly, wisely, and wholly without prejudice or fantasy any practical question which might come up. .So happy and contented a disposition, so tender and self-sacrificing a spirit, and so sure and well-balanced a judgment in the ordinary affairs of life as he possessed could only be understood in his home; and his richest influence was felt by those whose lives were closely bound up with his own. . . . One of his most remarkable qualities, considering his birth and nurture and personal tastes, was the intense sympathy he felt for the working classes. Labor, not as a means towards the mere making of money, but in itself, he esteemed in a characteristically American way; and his respect for working men in general was extended to individuals, and was quickly felt by all of humbler birth with whom he came in contact. . . . The bent of his mind was primarily scientific and practical; but he had a keen feeling for literature and for music, and an infinite respect for all forms of art."

Died at New Brunswick, N. J., March 5, 1884.

Married, in Dresden, Saxony, April 14, 1873, Mariana Alley Griswold, eldest daughter of George Griswold of New York.

Issue:

1. George Griswold Van Rensselaer, b. in New Brunswick, N. J., February 11, 1875. After preparatory studies in Dresden and New York he entered Harvard University, 1892; d. at Colorado Springs, Col., April 22, 1894. A relative communicates the following: "Short though his life was, it had fulfilled its early promise, and the fine and engaging qualities of his nature are held in enduring remembrance by many."